Voices of the Left Behind

Olga Rains, Lloyd Rains, and Melynda Jarratt

Voices of the Left Behind

Project Roots
and the
Canadian War Children
of World War II

THE DUNDURN GROUP
TORONTO

Copy-Editor: Lloyd Davis
Design: Andrew Roberts
Printer: Marquis

Library and Archives Canada Cataloguing in Publication

Rains, Olga
   Voices of the left behind : Project Roots and the Canadian war children of World War II / Olga Rains, Lloyd Rains and Melynda Jarratt.

First ed. published Fredericton, N.B. : Project Roots, 2004.

Includes bibliographical references.

ISBN 10: 1-55002-585-6
ISBN 13: 978-1-55002-585-9

   1. Illegitimate children--Netherlands--Biography. 2. Children of military personnel--Netherlands--Biography. 3. Children of military personnel--Canada--Biography. 4. World War, 1939-1945--Children--Netherlands--Biography. 5. Project Roots. 6. Netherlands--Biography. I. Rains, Lloyd II. Jarratt, Melynda III. Project Roots IV. Title.

D810.C4R34 2006   940.53'161'0922   C2005-906956-2

1   2   3   4   5   10   09   08   07   06

We acknowledge the support of the Canada Council for the Arts and the Ontario Arts Council for our publishing program. We also acknowledge the financial support of the Government of Canada through the Book Publishing Industry Development Program and The Association for the Export of Canadian Books, and the Government of Ontario through the Ontario Book Publishers Tax Credit program, and the Ontario Media Development Corporation.

Care has been taken to trace the ownership of copyright material used in this book. The author and the publisher welcome any information enabling them to rectify any references or credit in subsequent editions.

J. Kirk Howard, President

Printed and bound in Canada.
Printed on recycled paper.

www.dundurn.com

Dundurn Press	Gazelle Book Services Limited	Dundurn Press
3 Church Street, Suite 500	White Cross Mills	2250 Military Road
Toronto, Ontario, Canada	Hightown, Lancaster, England	Tonawanda NY
M5E 1M2	LA1 4X5	U.S.A. 14150

Voices of the Left Behind

Table of Contents

Acknowledgements

Voices of the Left Behind is a unique mixture of personal narratives, oral histories, original photographs and documents that were gathered over the course of nearly twenty-five years by Olga and Lloyd Rains, founders of the Dutch-based Project Roots. Together with co-editor Melynda Jarratt in New Brunswick, Canada, the Rains worked via e-mail from their home in Haarlem, the Netherlands, for more than three years to bring these stories to life, choosing the stories, gathering the images and documents, getting permission from each participant, translating, editing, rewriting and sometimes rewriting a story again if necessary. This is truly a book that would not have been possible without the Internet.

Each chapter contains an introductory essay that provides a social, cultural and historical context for the war-child story, from the experiences of war children in Britain, Holland, Belgium or Germany to the unique circumstances facing war children who were adopted at birth, whose fathers were Native Canadians, whose mothers were war brides, or whose mothers were Canadian servicewomen stationed overseas during the war. Using original sources found in the Public Archives of Canada and elsewhere, these introductions — and the final chapter, "By Virtue of His Service" — are a call to action and serve to shed light on a heretofore-unknown part of our Canadian history. The Rains and Ms. Jarratt sincerely hope this book will motivate a student of history to pursue the subject of the Canadian war children and their treatment since the end of World War II as the basis of a master's or doctoral thesis. Certainly, there are considerable gaps in our understanding of this period, and much research remains to be done in the Public Archives of Canada as well as in England and Holland if we are to fully understand the war-child story and the place it holds in our country's history.

Many thousands of hours of volunteer work has gone into the production of this book, and for this the Rains and Ms. Jarratt have numerous persons to acknowledge. Thanks are due to George Butters, who faithfully guided the editing of the book; Bill Traer, for his amazing patience and skill; Jan Walker, for her editing skills, sharp eye and encouragement over the past few years; and Patsy Hennessy, for her careful edit of the final manuscript.

Most importantly, however, this book would never have been published if not for the courage of the Canadian war children, their mothers in Britain and Europe, as well as the war children's relatives in Canada and others who contributed their stories, pictures and documents to bring this story to life. In alphabetical order, they are:

Alma
Margaret Atkinson
Sheila Blake
Richard Bond
Johnny Bruggenkamp
Winnie Bullen
Robert Burwell
Celestine
Chris
Karen (Flintoff) Cockwell
Christine Coe
Sandra (Campbell) Connor
Diane
Elly
Eloise
Maureen Fletcher
Alan Franklin
Simonne Gallis
Josephine Gee
Carol Anne Hobbs
Peter Hurricks
Jill
John
Willy Joormans

Irene Lynk
Diane and Ron Matthews
Nano Pennefeather-McConnell
Jenny Moore
Mary K.
Pat K.
Katja
Joan Kramer-Potts
Mia
Mira
Nel
Peter
Kathleen Swann
Leona Tange
Hans Kingma
Ralph Thompson
Sally
Theo Timmer
Willy Van Ee
Jan Walker
Pamela Walker
Susanne Werth
Christine Wilson
Heiko Windels

Lloyd and Olga Rains and Melynda Jarratt, September 2003.

Preface

As president of the Transatlantic Children's Enterprise (TRACE) and, at the beginning, the receiver of all enquiries, I was very glad to learn of Project Roots in Holland.

Our expertise was confined to advising on the search for American GIs; therefore, being able to pass on requests for help in finding Canadian fathers who had been in Europe in World War II to Olga Rains was a great help.

My involvement with this work began with the publication of my first book, *Sentimental Journey: The story of the GI Brides,* in 1984. One chapter, "Lost and Found," related to the efforts of people, not always deliberately left behind, to find their GI fathers. Letters from people in similar situations began to pour in.

The late Pamela Winfield.

At first, I could use only my own knowledge of the United States, the fact that I had been a military wife, and the efforts of friends in the U.S. to help them. Then came a breakthrough, courtesy of the Ralph Nader Association in the U.S. One of the GI babies took the U.S. government to court to allow them access to military records and won. As long as they had such basic information as a full name, and the dates their fathers were in the U.K., these people were entitled to his last known address.

This was only the beginning, but now, with the advent of facilities on the Internet, we have had a large number of successes. Rarely are they rejected.

On the wall of my office are photographs of GI fathers with their British children. Much to my delight, their numbers continue to grow.

I can only hope, for the sake of the Canadian children, they will get the same official assistance.

Pamela Winfield, MBE
President of TRACE

[Note: Pamela Winfield passed away in October 2004. The authors are grateful that she was able to contribute this preface.]

Chapter 1

The Canadians in Britain, 1939–1946
by Melynda Jarratt

"They're oversexed, overpaid, and over here!"

King George inspects Canadian troops at the army base in Croydon, England, during World War II, date unknown. The Canadians spent more time in England than any of the other Allied troops. Of 48,000 war brides, 44,000 were from Britain, the majority of whom came to Canada after the war and settled here. But the Canadians also left behind an estimated 23,000 war children from relationships they had with single and married women in the U.K.

"They're oversexed, overpaid, and over here!" Well-known comedian Tommy Trinder touched a nerve in British society when he uttered those famous words during World War II.[1] Intended to be a gibe at American GIs who were romancing British women, the saying could easily apply to the Canadians, whose stay in Britain exceeded the GIs' by more than two years.

Between 1939 and 1945, nearly half a million Canadian soldiers poured into Great Britain. Most of them were concentrated in southern England, and some who arrived in Aldershot in 1939 spent up to six years in the area. Naturally, the Canadians met British women, and whenever that happened there was romance and its inevitable results.

Forty-four thousand Canadian servicemen married British women during the war,[2] but a large number also had relationships with local women — some brief affairs, others long term — which resulted in the birth of an estimated 23,000[3] illegitimate[4] children whom we know as the British war children of World War II.

A homecoming party for a soldier back from Europe, at the Club Venetian, Montreal, December, 1945. When the Canadians came home, girlfriends left behind were easily forgotten.

Although the terms "illegitimate" and "bastard" no longer apply today, they were once powerful social statements on the position of unwed mothers and what their fatherless children could expect in British society. Marginalized and disenfranchised by virtue of their marital and birth status, both mothers and war children were treated with derision and received little, if any, sympathy or support from either side, British or Canadian. (See Chapter 8 for further discussion of this issue.)

Unlike the war brides who married their Canadian boyfriends and came to Canada to live at the end of the war, these women were abandoned by their soldier boyfriends, now officially Canadian veterans, who disappeared off the face of the earth once they returned to Canada at the end of the war. Desperate pleas to the Canadian military authorities, Veterans Affairs and External Affairs as to the whereabouts of missing fathers were fruitless — and continue to be to this day under the pretext of Canada's Privacy Act.

Left alone to raise their children in a highly judgmental, moralistic society, often without financial support or skills, many women decided to give up their children for adoption or were forced to hand them over to relatives. And at a time when there were few social supports or economic opportunities for women, those who decided to go it on their own suffered enormous social consequences that still reverberate in the lives of the war children today.

John Costello, in his famous study of changing social values during World War II titled *Love, Sex and War*, describes these British women and the wartime circumstances that found them unwed and pregnant with the children of foreign soldiers:

> Of the 5.3 million British infants delivered between 1939 and 1945, over a third were illegitimate — and this wartime phenomenon was not confined to any one section of society. The babies that were born out of wedlock belonged to every age group of mother, concluded one social researcher.
>
> Some were adolescent girls who had drifted away from homes which offered neither guidance nor warmth and security. Still others were women with husbands on war service, who had been unable to bear the loneliness of separation. There were decent and serious, superficial and flighty, irresponsible and incorrigible girls among them. There were some who had formed serious attachments and hoped to marry. There were others who had a single lapse, often under the influence of drink. There were, too, the "good-time girls" who thrived on the presence of well-paid servicemen from overseas, and semi-prostitutes with little moral restraint. But for the war many of these girls, whatever their type, would never have had illegitimate children.[5]

One of the most famous war children is legendary blues guitarist Eric Clapton, who discovered in March 1998, that his father, Edward Fryer, was a soldier from Montreal. Raised by his grandparents as their son, Clapton found out when he was nine that his sister Patricia was actually his mother. His story of a lifelong search for a Canadian father he never knew is one that echoes loudly for the British war children of World War II.

NOTES

1 Trinder is widely credited for the famous saying "They're overpaid, oversexed, and over here!", intended as a gibe against American servicemen in Europe.

2 Immigration Branch, Annual Report of the Department of Mines and Resources 1947–48 (Ottawa: Edmund Cloutier, King's Printer, 1948), p. 240. As cited in Melynda Jarratt, *The War Brides of New Brunswick*, master's report (Fredericton: University of New Brunswick, 1995), p. 5.

3 This is a an estimate of Canadian war children born in Britain. Recent correspondence (December 2003) with the Public Records Office, the National Archives and the Office of National Statistics in the U.K. confirm that evidence of Canadian paternity found in the birth certificates for illegitimate children born during the war years has never been compiled and is therefore unavailable at this time. It has also been suggested that the number of children whose fathers were Canadian servicemen may never be known; married women whose British husbands were away during the war would have given their Canadian children their husband's name, as opposed to the biological father's name. We know this to be the case for several children whose stories appear in this book. The lack of readily available statistical evidence points to a need for further research in the British archives to determine through objective analysis the numbers of war children whose fathers were Canadian servicemen.

4 We used the word "illegitimate" only to separate children born out of wedlock from those whose parents were legally married. It by no means carries the social stigma it did as recently as ten years ago.

5 John Costello, *Love Sex and War: Changing Values 1939-45* (London: Collins, 1985), pp. 276–77.

Exceeded All My Hopes
by John*

I was born at the end of 1946 in London, England, to an English mother and a Canadian soldier who had returned to Canada with his regiment in the middle of 1946. The months leading up to and immediately after my birth were very difficult for my mother. She was sent to a Roman Catholic home for unmarried mothers. After I was born, a charitable organization arranged for her to work as home help with a Roman Catholic couple in Sussex.

In 1947, my grandfather returned from naval service and set up home near Portsmouth in Hampshire, so I went to live with my grandparents. My mother, meanwhile, had managed to get office work in Sussex, and came to see us on the weekends. My grandfather's home was a small holding in the countryside, and I have fond memories of this early period in my life. I also established a strong bond with my grandfather.

My mother met and married my stepfather in 1948. He was serving with the Royal Air Force, and I continued to live with my grandparents until he was posted to Nairobi in East Africa in 1949. I went abroad with my mother, and then was formally adopted by my stepfather when we returned to England in 1953.

I had a happy childhood, and my mother ensured that I acquired a good education. At age twenty-six I married and settled in Lincolnshire, where we have lived ever since. We have had two children of our own, who gave my mother much joy up to her death in 1992. My stepfather followed her shortly after in 1994.

All in all I have been fortunate and had a good life with no regrets, but I have always wondered about my Canadian father. With both my parents gone, in 1995 I decided to find out more about my biological father's background. I had little information to go on: a name, the fact that he had been a Canadian soldier, and that he had been awarded a medal for bravery.

I began my research in the London archives and also made contact with Olga Rains at Project Roots. Olga was immensely supportive, and encouraged me with advice although, at that time, I had no real facts on which to base a search. Eventually I was able to link the name and the medal, and to acquire a copy of the military citation. Being a wartime citation, it did not, of course, contain any personal information, but it did provide me with a regiment and service number.

This was the breakthrough that Olga needed, and with her extensive contacts in Canada she was able to trace my father in a very short time. At the end of 1999 she telephoned my father on my behalf, and so initiated a relationship for which I am eternally in her debt.

For two years we corresponded and spoke on the telephone, getting to know each other and coming to terms with an almost miraculous reunion.

At the end of 2001 I retired from a working life of travel abroad, and in the summer of 2002 my wife and I visited Canada to meet my father. I do not possess the literary skills to describe how much it meant to both of us. Suffice it to say it was a memorable trip. We visited the places of my father's childhood, and he provided me with a wealth of background information on my roots.

I can say that the whole experience has exceeded by far any hopes that I might have had when I embarked on my search, and I cannot thank Olga and everybody at Project Roots enough.

*John is a pseudonym

Still He Eludes Me
by Sheila Blake

My name is Sheila Blake (née Shoulders). I was born in England on March 3, 1944, in the small village of Shottermill, near Haslemere, Surrey, in a beautiful house called Ridgecomb.

I was thirty-seven years old when I first heard that my father was a Canadian. Although it was a shock, in retrospect I was not the least surprised.

My mother's name was Eileen Patricia Ayling. During the war, she lived at Park Road as well as Worthing and Dolphin Road, Shoreham-by-Sea, Sussex, where I was raised.

I believe my Canadian father, Gavin McGuire or McGurk (spelling?), may have been based in Surrey, probably Hindhead. His uniform indicates he was

Sheila Blake's father, Gavin McGuire or McGurk, may have been an engineer with the Royal Canadian Engineers. He joined up in Edmonton, Alberta.

an engineer and served with the Royal Canadian Engineers; however, he was also known as Gunner McGurk, possibly because he was initially with the Royal Canadian Edmonton Regiment (Artillery).

He was six feet tall, red-headed and very well built. His eyes were blue. Not surprisingly, my son has red hair and a lazy eye, just like my father and myself. I know what he looks like, but am uncertain of his name. An elderly family member told me my father was Gavin McGuire or McGurk and that he came from Edmonton, Alberta.

Apparently, my father was badly injured during the D-Day landings and was shipped back to Saskatchewan. His mother wrote to my family with news of his condition, as she was concerned he would not recover from a severe head injury.

I've been told he survived the war and returned to the U.K. to be reunited with my mother and me. However, my mother had already married Frank Shoulders and was pregnant with my brother, so she stayed with her husband.

The portrait of my natural father came into my possession in November 1999, while I was visiting my family in Sussex, England.

My mother passed away in 1985, and before she died I believe she tried to tell me something about my father. However, she was so heavily sedated with morphine that she was unable to bring the memories back.

When I finally saw my father's portrait fourteen years later, it dawned on me what she had been trying to say on her deathbed. I've just become a grandmother, and my grandson is the image of the man in the photo.

I do hope someone will recognize my father's picture. I have a file that is now a good four inches thick, but am no nearer to discovering his whereabouts. It seems unbelievable that I can have a photo clearly showing his uniform and regimental badge, a probable name, a U.K. location during the war, and yet still he eludes me.

Sheila and her mother, Patricia Ayling. Sheila's father was injured in the D-Day landings and was shipped back to Saskatchewan. In his absence, Patricia married another man in England.

Better Off without Him
by Alan Franklin

Alan Franklin is the editor of the Surrey-Hants Star in Aldershot, England. His Canadian father has refused contact.

The ironic thing about my Canadian father is that sixty years ago he was stationed in the area where I now edit the local newspaper, writing stories about Canadian fathers who abandoned their British offspring sixty years ago.

I was born on February 11, 1946, exactly nine months after Victory in Europe Day, May 8, 1945. I was a victory celebration baby, born into austere postwar Britain, where cold houses, rationing and shortages of everything were our way of life.

Meanwhile, back in Canada with his English wife, my father Patrick Johnson (not his real name) was setting out on a successful career which ended, I am told, with him working as head foreman of the Vancouver water company. He had four children, two boys and two girls, one of them born around the same time as me.

My mother had married another Canadian soldier, Corporal Franklin of the Paratroop Regiment, who also swiftly followed the pattern of the abandonment of British wives and girlfriends at the war's end. So we were left to manage as best we could, my mother working at the post office telegrams department, doing administration for the Surrey Police and other office jobs to support us both. Meanwhile my grandmother kept house and cooked meals for my mother and me, my grandfather (a steam-engine driver) and my aunt (a civil servant).

Single parenthood was not fashionable then, and I knew no other boy without a father present. Sometimes I wondered who and where he was, but questions were discouraged and I just got on with my life until, in my teens, as a young reporter, I interviewed a private detective. This man traced missing relatives. I asked him to trace Corporal Reginald Franklin, not knowing then that he was not my real father. He did, with a "last trace" of him detected through a contact with the Canadian Legion.

When I revealed my research to my mother she was horrified; Franklin was even more of a dead loss than Johnson, whose last communication with my mother, some months before I was born, was a card posted from Canada in 1945 "wishing you well next year" — at my birth. This was the full extent of Johnson's help to his secret English family.

My attempt at tracing Franklin flushed out the hitherto-unsuspected existence of Johnson. My mother was a little hazy about where he had come from and, Canada being a large country, I presumed I had no hope of finding him, so I forgot all about it until 1984, when I had just been appointed to my present job as editor of the *Surrey and Hants Star* in Aldershot, Hampshire, England.

Stories of the Canadian war children appear frequently in the Surrey-Hants Star.

My colleague John Walton, an experienced journalist and formerly the deputy editor of *Soldier Magazine*, also based in Aldershot, said he was off on a trip to Canada and would look up Johnson in the phone book. As he was headed for Vancouver he immediately discovered P. Johnson — there was just one in the phone book — and returned with his address. I then wrote a simple letter to my father, asking him to get in touch. He never did, although he subsequently claimed that a letter had been sent to me and that he even tried to visit me at my home in Alton, Hampshire.

This seemed unlikely, as I have never been hard to trace, being a well-known local journalist all my adult life, with my byline and picture appearing in papers going through tens of thousands of doors. Additionally, when I was a reporter I called every day at all the local police stations, so I was not exactly unknown to them! Neither did a letter come back marked "address unknown," so my letter was certainly delivered.

Having deduced that my father didn't want to know me, I again got on with my life, enjoying my family and career. Then, in 1998, Mark Maclay wrote a book called *Aldershot's Canadians*, which told the stories of the 330,000 Canadian servicemen stationed in the

Aldershot area during the war years. I reviewed it and sent a copy to Lloyd and Olga Rains, whom I knew as the couple who discovered fathers of war babies.

This was now the computer age and everybody, more or less, was easily traceable. It took Olga just a few minutes on her computer to come up with the address of several Johnsons, one of them my cousin Linda who, in turn, led me to my dad.

Linda and another cousin, Jeff, were friendly and helpful. I sent Linda pictures showing the family likeness, which I think is obvious, and saying that if there was any doubt I would happily arrange a DNA test, which I subsequently tried to do. But I hadn't reckoned on the cold refusal of my father to show any interest in me, or agree to anything which a court didn't order.

To say he didn't want to know was an understatement: Linda told me he was a Shriner (a branch of Freemasonry) and a member of the Lutheran Church, and it was obvious that the last thing he wanted was me rattling a few skeletons round his doorstep. I thanked Linda for not doubting me and explained all the reasons why I was telling the truth. If I had wanted a "Canadian family" or to live in Canada, I already had my birth certificate stating that I was the son of a Canadian serviceman — my mother's husband Franklin. So I could get a Canadian passport at any time. Because I am married to an American I could also get U.S. residency and, eventually, citizenship, so I was not motivated by a desire to move to Canada.

As for money, my wife and I presumed that if we ever traced my father he would probably be a bum on the streets. What other kind of man would abandon an unborn child and never inquire as to his welfare? In our view, he would need *our* help, not the other way around, and our help would have been gladly given.

I had two phone conversations with Patrick Johnson at that time, both of which were a trifle odd. He claimed to have flown to Britain with his wife in 1984 or 1985 and spent some time looking for me, even asking the police my whereabouts. We moved from the home in Alton, from which I had written the letter, in 1985, but we sold the house to close friends who could have located me in two minutes. I also told him in my letter that I edited the local paper, so finding me would not have taxed Sherlock Holmes. Mr. Johnson also claimed his wife has written me a letter, but I didn't receive it. Very odd.

In his first phone call he said coldly, "I am not your father" — which begs the question of why he would claim to have tried to find me. After his first phone call, I dashed over to Guildford to talk to my mother and she was contemptuous of his denials.

I called him back and he said something that struck me as curious: "I can't change my story now." He admitted he had "been intimate" with my mother, but claimed it was only before his wedding in December 1943. My mother disputes this and says that in 1944, when both she and Patrick operated different switchboards in the Farnborough area, Patrick chatted to her and asked her over to the Canadian hospital to meet him. This led to their affair, which lasted some time. She was then posted away, and they resumed their relationship in 1945. She says he was aware she was pregnant and sent her the postcard wishing her luck.

Patrick claimed to know the name of my "real father" but wouldn't reveal it. How this ties in with his claim that he didn't see my mother after his marriage, I don't know... I think that Patrick is ashamed of "playing around" shortly after his wedding. Had my conception happened first, perhaps he would have admitted it. However, the dates make him look bad, and he is ashamed to admit fathering me.

He promised to see me when he next came to England, in the summer of 1999, but I felt this was too long to wait. Foolishly, in 1998 I wrote a long and detailed letter to Johnson about my life, hoping this would interest him in my family. Instead, he has subsequently used it to make unpleasant points about me.

I last spoke to Patrick Johnson on September 3, 1999, when the phone rang at home at 9:30 p.m. He had been on his annual summer trip to the Isle of Wight, an island off the coast of Britain, where his first wife came from. He stays there with his late wife's sister, who, I understand, lives in a house bought by Johnson.

He was calling from Liphook, a village in Hampshire around thirty miles from where we live in Fleet. But even though I could have been there in under an hour, he refused to allow me to come and meet him. This was the only time I felt really upset at his attitude: I knew this would be my only chance to see him, because of his advancing years and because he had already warned me not to call on him in Canada.

Had I known where he was calling from, I would have driven there anyway, but he was careful not to reveal this, although he said he was staying with relatives of his first wife. Mr. Johnson told me he was getting a lift to the airport in the morning to fly home to Canada. I begged him to see me, but he hadn't the guts to do so, despite having promised that he would — a promise he had used simply to buy some more time.

He was very cold, guarded and kept trying to ring off. He did say he was making a tape about his wartime affair with my mother, which he would send me and also make available to his children on his death. He said he had consulted a solicitor on the Isle of Wight, and he expected a response from me once I had heard the tape. His prime interest seemed to be in limiting any possible damage to his precious reputation.

A Canadian soldier arrives in Canada after five long years overseas. Who knows if he left a child behind?

When I got the tape I decided I would make no further effort to contact Johnson. It contained a ridiculous, one-sided attempt at smearing my mother — the only person who kept me out of an orphanage — and was full of self-justification and excuses. It is one of the most disgusting statements I have ever heard, an opinion shared by the Rains, who could scarcely believe their ears. It seems, you see, that this strapping Canadian soldier was entirely overpowered and seduced by this little seven-stone, five-foot Englishwoman. What a terrible experience it must have been for him. I am surprised he didn't seek immediate counselling.

So much for Johnson. The good news was that cousin Linda came over with her new husband, Bart, and spent her honeymoon with us in Hampshire in 2004!

Linda and Bart are a wonderful, outgoing Canadian couple and we spent some happy days seeing the sights and showing them England, where Linda's father and uncles had spent their wartime years.

Our children, Daniel and Anne, at last had some relatives to relate to on my father's side, where previously there had been a void. We have kept in touch since their return to Canada and we have a standing invitation to visit them.

Linda also brought loads of family history and pictures with her: at last my German/Canadian roots were revealed!

I phoned my half-brother Dale, in Ottawa, but he showed no interest, so at the time of writing Linda and Bart *are* our Canadian family. We are delighted to know them, and even if we never meet any other "Johnsons," we will have succeeded in expanding our family in a wonderful way.

Awkward Moments
by Celestine

At the end of March 1989, I flew to Toronto to meet my Canadian father, Louis, for the first time. During the whole flight I was so nervous and the same thoughts kept racing through my mind. Did I look like him? I was not as good-looking as my English mother, Libby. She had beautiful long, curly, blonde hair and dark-brown eyes. I was just a plain dark blonde with straight hair cut in a bob.

I had seen a photo of Louis in the service, a handsome young soldier, but he never did send me a photo of how he looked now. So I tried to draw a picture in my mind: maybe his hair was all grey or white, or maybe he had no hair at all? Were his eyes like mine — not blue and not green, sort of in between?

It was not his fault that he couldn't raise me: it was Libby's. She left my father when she became pregnant. Libby didn't love him the way he loved her. She was so young, only seventeen years old. My grandparents raised me, so I grew up thinking they were my parents and Libby was my sister.

I found out much later that Louis wanted to marry Libby, but my grandparents were against it. Besides, she didn't really care about Louis. Libby liked to have fun, go out, and be carefree, and she did until she was in a bad accident that left her disabled.

As I walked through the doors at the airport and saw all the people who were waiting to welcome their families and friends, I wondered how I would find my father. As I stood there, a well-dressed man came towards me with a big bouquet of roses. It was Louis, my father. He put his arms around me and held me tight. The tears kept streaming down my face. We were both very emotional as we walked down the parking lot to where his car was.

This first visit with my Canadian father was a strange and emotional time. At first he wanted to see me as his "girlfriend" — and, more importantly, wanted other people to believe that this was so. Apart from his ego, he had great difficulty explaining me to friends, and there were quite a few awkward moments.

I could appreciate his discomfort, but I had spent the whole of my childhood in situations where no one wanted to say who I was, and there was no way I was going to put up with that at the age of forty-five.

So, initially, we had conflicts over his feelings towards me, what he wanted from me, and what I felt I could give. But we got along so well and I knew that he loved me and was proud of me.

When he became ill, I nursed him and worried over him. I stayed for a few days with my husband's relations in Montreal, and this gave me the opportunity to talk to someone from outside the situation. I realized that Louis was terrified of losing me, the way he had lost my mother, his first and only love. This made him demanding and sometimes very difficult. I realized how much I missed him, and when I returned I was more confident and able to laugh at his "grumpy" ways.

I returned to Toronto for three weeks in May and we had a lovely time together. In July, my father came to us — something he had said he would never do. He stayed for ten weeks. He became a part of my family and I was really happy. He was spoiled and did not want to return to Canada.

I had not been prepared for how desolate I felt when he left, and I realized how important it is that we make the most of the time left to us. We made enquiries about him living with us, and it appears that he is not eligible, so we have to fight. He very much wants to come and stay with us. He is a very lonely man; he never married and has no family anymore.

I realize now that my father and I have a more intense relationship than most people under normal circumstances, but as long as he is happy and my husband, children and I are happy, then it doesn't really matter what the rest of the world thinks.

Sometimes I think I am dreaming. That I could have found a father who loves me, hugs me and laughs and cries with me is more than I had ever hoped for.

Many young soldiers wanted a relationship with the mothers of their children but it was not meant to be.

His Father's Eyes
by Melynda Jarratt

The most famous Canadian war child is legendary blues-rock guitarist Eric Clapton, whose father was a soldier from Montreal named Edward Fryer.

Clapton was born on March 30, 1945, to Patricia Molly Clapton, a sixteen-year-old English teenager whose brief relationship with the piano-playing soldier from Quebec resulted in pregnancy.

Raised by his grandparents, Eric was nine years old when he found out that his sister Patricia was actually his mother, but all he ever knew about his father was the name Edward Fryer and some rumours that he was involved in banking. He wasn't even sure of the spelling: was it Fryer or Friar?

Project Roots first became involved in the search for Eric Clapton's father in September 1997, when Lloyd and Olga Rains were contacted by an English lawyer who asked for information on the Canadian soldier Edward Fryer or Friar. The lawyer would not reveal his client's name, only that he wanted information on Fryer.

The Rains had never heard of Eric Clapton, so the name Fryer meant nothing to them. They conducted a regular search and sent off the information to the lawyers. Little did they know that at the same they were looking for Canadian veteran Edward Fryer, so too was Michael Woloschuk, a writer for the *Ottawa Citizen* whose parallel search superseded Project Roots and ended up on the front pages of every major newspaper in the world in March 1998.

In an article in the *Citizen* on March 26, 1998, Woloschuk explained that he began looking for Edward Fryer in the fall of 1997, urged on by a friend who knew Clapton was planning a North American tour in March to promote his latest album, *Pilgrim*. Clapton was Woloschuk's musical hero and, like anybody else who had read the musician's 1985 biography, he knew that Clapton's father was a Canadian soldier named Edward Fryer. He knew, too, that Clapton had never been able to find the man.

With the death in 1991 of Clapton's five-year-old son, Conor, and the success of *Pilgrim*'s hit single, the sad but hopeful "My Father's Eyes," it seemed the right time for Woloschuk to use his journalistic connections to find Edward Fryer. He was right.

Six months later, on the eve of Clapton's North American tour, the front-page article in the *Citizen* told the world about Eric Clapton's father, a talented musician and artist who died of leukemia in a Toronto veteran's hospital in 1985. Fryer was also a marrying man who left behind a trail of wives and children across Canada and the United States. Three half-brothers and sisters, from British Columbia to Florida, were thrilled to find out about their connection with Eric Clapton.

The story spread rapidly across North America, Britain and Europe. In an interview with the *Toronto Sun* the next day, Clapton was quoted as being pleased, if not a little irritated, that the family he had sought for so long was discovered by a Canadian newspaper reporter.

"First of all, I was furious that I have to find this stuff out through a newspaper. I think it was very intrusive — but then, newspapers are," Clapton told the *Sun*. "Then I thought, this is great. The upside, the positive, is that it supplied me with information I'd never had before."

According to the article, Fryer was cremated and his ashes were scattered off Florida waters by his last love, Sylvia (Goldie) Nickason, an Ontario woman with whom Fryer spent his last years.

The Rains' involvement in the search for Edward Fryer had begun inauspiciously enough six months earlier, when they received their first correspondence from the English law firm. As she had done for so many others, Olga wrote back to the lawyer and said they would do a search, and she eventually sent along a list of sixteen addresses for E. Fryer or E. Friar. As is the case with so many other requests from lawyers, once the law firm got the information, Olga never heard from them again — not even to thank her for the list of names.

"It's typical," Olga says. "As soon as they get what they want, we never hear from them again, but we get used to it. It's discouraging sometimes, but you don't let it bother you. There are too many good people out there who appreciate what we do, and besides, we can always hope that the information we provided helped the war child find his father, and that would mean something good came out of our work even if we never find out about it."

Months passed, and Olga never gave the request another thought. Other cases came up and she put the letters aside with the intention of recycling them, but somehow the correspondence survived.

In the meantime, unbeknownst to the Rains or to Clapton's lawyers, Woloschuk was making headway with his own search. Olga says she will "never forget the day" they got the call from Canada saying that there was a big article in the *Ottawa Citizen* about this famous musician named Eric Clapton and his Canadian father, a veteran named Edward Fryer.

"I knew about Fryer, as we had done the search six months previously, but I said, 'So who is this Eric Clapton?' We're old people; we don't know anything about rock 'n' roll music!"

Once they got over the surprise of learning the identity of the anonymous figure to whose lawyer they had provided a list of names and addresses, the Rains wrote the law firm, informing them that, with the *Citizen* article, the cat was now out of the bag. The Rains said they knew the anonymous client was Eric Clapton, and although they were very happy for him, they had never received as much as a thank-you for their efforts.

Less than a week later, a letter arrived at their doorstep, with a donation to Project Roots and a special thank-you from the lawyer: "I would like personally, and on behalf of our Client, to thank you for your assistance."

After so many twists and turns, it was a fitting end to the search for a Canadian soldier whose son just happens to be one of the most famous musicians in the world today.

Mixed Blessings
by Olga Rains

Christine Wilson's father was a Canadian serviceman who returned to England after the war. Her mother, Patricia Swallow, met Robert Cater in London and, according to a family member who had a very brief glimpse of Cater on one occasion, they had a short relationship.

Patricia could not take care of her daughter, so when Christine was two years old she was sent to an orphanage and later to foster homes. At age four, she was brought back into the fold when her mother married. The reunion was short: three years later, when Christine was seven, Patricia Swallow died. Raised by her stepfather, Christine was thirteen when she was told the truth about her biological father.

Not knowing her real father and having been with her mother for such a short time left huge gaps in Christine's sense of identity. It also made her search for her roots all the more important. She contacted Project Roots and we set about looking for her Canadian family.

Soon we found Christine's half-brother in Canada. He was thrilled to hear about his English sister, and he had quite a story to tell about their father.

It seems that Robert Cater was a married man with four young children when he went to England during World War II. When he returned to Canada, he wanted his family to move to England with him. His eldest son, being eleven years old at the time, remembers that his mother did not want to go, so his father went to England alone, leaving his Canadian family behind. In England, the father had a short relationship with Christine's mother. He

After being an only child for so long, Christine Wilson now has two lovely families, one in Canada, another in Australia, who have accepted her into their lives.

also had a relationship with another English woman, whom he married and had another family with. They emigrated to Australia in 1960.

When we found Christine's brother in Canada, we sent him a photo. He wrote the following letter back to us.

> Received your letter with Christine's photo, she resembles my sisters, her posture and her looks, especially when my sisters were younger. You can give Christine my address and phone number. I have two sisters and one brother. My younger sister would love to hear from Christine and so would I.

In her own words, Christine wrote the following letters to us describing her feelings and gratitude for our help in the search for her father:

> June 2000: I received a letter from my half-brother in Canada and have since spoken to him on the phone. I also wrote to my father in Australia who, because of his age (87) and the fact that he is finding the situation a bit overwelming (no surprise there, I suppose!), asked his eldest daughter from his Australian marriage to write back.
>
> I received a friendly letter from her. She is just nine months older than me and her brother and two sisters are younger. It is obvious that my father had an affair with my mother whilst he was married to his second wife.
>
> The children were all born in London, England, and they emigrated to Australia in 1960. I must admit that I had always assumed my father was a single man having a good time and did not want to be trapped when my mother became pregnant.
>
> What a shock and what a man!

> November 2000: My trip to Canada was a bit of a mixed blessing. I found it a bit overwhelming as there were so many of them and only one of me! I received a very warm welcome from everyone and I have made what I hope to be some lasting connections with some members of the family. I am in contact on a regular basis with my half-brother's two children.
>
> As for the family in Australia, I am in regular touch with them via e-mail and hope to visit there next year. My only regret is that I didn't do this years ago — but better late than never, I suppose.

It only remains for me to let you know how very, very grateful I am to you both for carrying out this search for me — I think my life can never be the same again! It must give you both an enormous amount of satisfaction to reunite so many families and indeed to see so many errant fathers face up to their past, if not the responsibility for their past. Many thanks. Christine.

Postscript: In April 2002, Christine went to Australia, where she had a warm welcome from her father's family. She stayed with her eldest sister and met with all the others and enjoyed the country very much.

Unfortunately, there was one other member of the family she did not meet, and that was her father. His health had been very fragile for over a year and he was almost ninety-one years old when he passed away, only a few weeks after Christine booked her flight.

Christine Wilson (right) with her Canadian family.

Canadian Bastard
by Sandra Connor

I was born in July 1944, to a six-teen-year-old English girl and a Canadian serviceman named Duncan Thomas Campbell. My father was sent to the Sicily land-ings, and by the time he returned late in 1945 or early 1946, my birth mother had already found another soldier to comfort her. Unmarried, and pregnant again with her sec-ond child, she gave up the baby girl to strangers and I was brought up by my grandparents, who raised me as their own.

Living in a small village where Canadians had their medical army base, I suppose there were many of us, but we didn't know — and we certainly didn't know each other. But all the things you say on your Project Roots website are true for me — the "Canadian bastard" from whom very little was expected and very little given.

Being called a "Canadian bastard" was a painful experience that many war children recall with sadness to this day.

At the age of nineteen I went to Canada, and within three weeks I found my Canadian birth father in Toronto. We met, and I was intro-duced to his wife and my half-siblings. Unfortunately, he died when I was travelling in Australia in 1968, and over time I lost touch with his family.

I now live in Canada and am the mother of two adopted boys in their early twenties. We do research into family trees and I find that I cannot get any information on my Canadian father as I have no legal right to his files. I know that he came from Nova Scotia, and that's as far as it goes. I suppose that I should count myself lucky that we met, and I do. But I was too young to appreciate the experience, and my father died before I had a chance to ask more meaningful questions.

I am now looking for my English half-sister, born in 1946 and given up for adoption by our birth mother. My sister may not even know that she is half-Canadian, but I have the name of her birth father, which may help in my search.

Looking back, I can say my life has been a success story. I live in Canada, am proud to be Canadian and, at the age of sixty-one, am glad to finally read about the terrible things we Canadian war children endured.

I am thankful to Project Roots for bringing the public's attention to our stories. We were the forgotten ones, unable to speak our thoughts for fear of upsetting our adoptive parents. What a pleasure to know we are really not "alone."

Looking for Harry Potter
by Christine Coe

I realized that I was different from other Irish kids at quite an early age. Their mums and dads were all younger than mine, their parents weren't so strict, and there was fun and laughter and hugs among them all.

Harry Potter, Christine's father, in a picture taken during World War II. Her mother last saw him in December 1943, and the last thing he said was, "I will return for you."

I still loved my five brothers and sisters and my parents, even though I was scared to death of my father. He was a very strict disciplinarian who thought nothing of beating me with a stick or shoe or whatever came to hand.

There was a real stigma surrounding any child who didn't have a dad, and I wasn't allowed to play with the little boy who lived down the road because he didn't have one. He was awful anyway, and was always fighting and calling my friends and me names.

One day when I was fourteen, I was standing at a table doing my homework. I looked out the window and saw that awful boy looking through our gate.

"What's that horrible boy looking in here for?" I asked my mum.

She replied that I shouldn't speak about him like that, as I wasn't any different. I looked at her in amazement. She went on to say that she had something to tell me: that I wasn't really her daughter — my eldest sister was my mum and she was my grandmother. My mind ran riot, all the lies, all the little digs from my "brothers and sisters." Now I understood why!

All they would tell me is that he was a Canadian pilot and he was killed in action during the war, but I didn't believe them. Somehow I was going to find my dad.

Well, their obedient, well-behaved daughter disappeared after that, and in her place was a rebellious, out-of-control teenager in the 1960s. When my "father" beat me I would scream at him that I would be happier dead and that he should kill me if that was what he really wanted.

I was packed off to England to live with my real mum when I was sixteen. By this time she had made her own life, and I wasn't part of it. She was good to me and bought me clothes and things, but she was terrified that someone would find out I was her daughter. She worked all hours, from early morning to late at night, so we hardly had any time to get to know each other.

Finally, one day I asked her about my dad. She told me he was a pilot and that he came from Montreal in Canada. Apparently he used to "borrow" a Leander aeroplane and dive and do loop-the-loops over her house on the weekends.

One day he crashed the plane in the field at the back of the house and was badly injured. My mum rescued him from the plane as he was unable to undo the seat belt and he had a badly injured leg and a head wound. He was court-martialled for this and sent to England for a time, but was then promoted to warrant officer and returned to Ireland.

My mum became pregnant with me and last saw him in December 1943, when she was four months pregnant. My dad was being sent home on medical grounds, but the last thing he said to her was "I will return for you."

She waited all her life — never married, never stopped loving him.

I continued to be a rebel, met my husband and had three sons. I tried various routes to find my father, writing letters to the Canadian Embassy, making contact with the Salvation Army. I even wrote to Cilla Black, the English television host whose program involves reuniting long-lost relatives.

One day I went to a medium, and she told me that my father had not passed over to the other side yet and that she could see him standing on a hill overlooking the countryside. She said there was water nearby, and that he was thinking about my mum and me and wondering what had happened to us.

I went away with renewed determination to find him. Reading a magazine one day, I saw an article about Project Roots and immediately sat down and wrote to the address they gave. They sent flyers out

Christine Coe was raised by her grandparents in Ireland. She found her father's family in Canada through the Project Roots website.

to all the Potters in Canada, then one day advised me to write to the Canadian archives and say that I was a "buddy" looking for a friend from the war years. I did this, and back came a reply with a special number to put on my envelope. It was really hard to write the letter, how do you introduce yourself — at forty-four years of age — to your father?

I was too late. Five months later, the letter was returned with "Deceased" written across it, but there were a few scribbled notes against some questions I had asked.

After this happened, Olga put my father's name up on their website (www.project-roots.com). I didn't know this had been done; I had given up hope and, although I had signed to give my permission, over the years I had forgotten all about it.

Out of the blue I received a telephone call from Olga saying that yes, my father was dead, but I had a half-sister who wanted to make contact.

I cannot describe the emotions I felt. The phone rang! It was my sister, Diane. I was shaking from head to toe; the atmosphere was electric. Tears streamed down my face when I heard her soft Canadian accent. I was forty-nine years old and speaking to my sister for the very first time.

Diane flew over to England the following month and stayed with my husband and me at our house. She told me about my three other sisters, that my dad had married at seventeen and later joined the war while her mom was pregnant with their third daughter.

My letter had arrived just three weeks after he died, and his wife opened it. She said nothing to her daughters about it for nearly a year, then told Diane. Diane started to look for my mum right away: She phoned every person in the telephone book with my mum's surname, but she was looking in Ireland — and, of course, both my mum and I lived in England.

One day she received a telephone call from her son to say he had been on the Internet: "Mom, Grandpa's name is on the Internet. Someone is looking for him ... an organization called Project Roots."

It has been an amazing two years. I have now met my sister Saundra and my niece Colleen and I e-mail my sister Suzanne all the time. Emotionally it has been hard, and I have cried so much I almost have shares in Kleenex. Happy tears and sad tears.

I have a wonderful, large family. I have pictures of my dad, and it's amazing to see the Potter family resemblance in me and my children and to know where my likes and dislikes come from.

At last I feel a whole person, not ashamed of who I am. I have the feeling of belonging, of knowing who I am.

He Was a Bigamist
by Olga Rains

Louis Burwell wrote many love letters to his English fiancée Sheila, and even though he often asked her to burn them, she never did. It's a good thing she didn't, because her son Robert would never have been able to trace Louis's Canadian family and find out what kind of man his father really was.

Louis Burwell in a wartime photo. Louis was already married in Canada when he married Robert Burwell's mother, Sheila, in England.

Sheila and Louis met in England in 1941, and what started as friendship soon turned into a love affair. But back in Canada, Louis had a wife named Florence and three young sons. That didn't stop him. On February 21, 1942, he and Sheila married, but since Louis hadn't bothered to obtain a divorce it was an illegal marriage and Louis was a bigamist. On October 6, 1944, a son Robert (Bob) was born in Salisbury, England. Like so many other Canadian servicemen, after the war Louis returned to Canada and was never seen or heard from again by his English wife and son.

Project Roots found out that Louis died on March 2, 1978, and was able to put Bob in touch with Tom, his half-brother. Tom was a teenager when his father went off to war, and his mother had told him all about the family Louis left behind in England. Tom was very anxious to meet Bob, and after many phone calls and letters, they finally connected in 2001.

Tom gave Bob a lot of mementos, including photos, maps and books that belonged to his father. The most precious gift that Tom gave him were Louis's three long-service medals. This means so much to Bob, to just hold them in his hands knowing that one time, long ago, Louis held them himself.

Incidentally, Louis's marriage in Canada nearly broke up at the time — no surprise, really — but eventually Florence and Louis made up and they stayed together for the rest of their lives.

For the full text of one of Louis Burwell's letters to Sheila, please refer to the Appendix (page 213).

I Found Real Happiness in Canada
by Jenny Moore

My father, John, was a Canadian soldier in World War II, and he spent time in England, where he met my mother, Joan, in Bournemouth.

John and Joan planned to marry, but I was born before that happened. John was of Ukrainian origin and his parents lived in Saskatchewan. My mother's parents were against the marriage, so they found a way to have John transferred to another part of England.

Thus began my unhappy life without a real mom or dad.

We lived with Gramma and Grampa until I was nine months old, when my mother married George, an Englishman. We moved to the house of George's parents for a while, then we moved again. We were very poor, and George would regularly come home drunk and beat up my mother.

George was sent away, Mom went to work, and things seemed to be better when suddenly Mom took me to Oxford, where George was living, and we moved back in with him. This only ended in more trouble. George had another woman, and life there was no different. One day we escaped to the police station, and since he couldn't hit my mother, he beat me up instead.

When I was six or seven I was sent to live with George. I never questioned the arrangement because I thought George was my real father. My main task there was to shine the brass outside the front door. I felt rejected and would wake up at night screaming from the nightmares.

One day Mom showed up with another man — Mike, an Irishman. He tried to be nice to me, but I rejected him and ran away. Life at home with George was awful and I spent much of my time on the streets. Believe me when I say I know what it is like to be hungry.

When I was nine, Mom showed up and took me to Banbury to live with a retired couple who were very nice to me. But I couldn't settle, so I wrote to George and he took me back to Oxford. Mom didn't like that, and eventually she took me away to live with her sister. I did not fit in and was unhappy there also.

In 1955, Mom picked me up to live with her and Mike, the Irishman, in Warwickshire. He told friends that I was his daughter. I didn't like that, plus Mike ruled with an iron rod and Mom didn't believe anything I told her, so there was a barrier between us.

I was not interested in school, so I dropped out. We moved to Warrington, where I worked at several different jobs and then I met a young man, we fell in love and I became pregnant. We eventually married, but this didn't last, either. I had a nervous breakdown, we broke up and I went to stay with my Aunt Joyce. During my time there, Aunt Joyce finally told me the big secret — my real father was a Canadian soldier! George was not my father after all. I was furious!

After years of searching we found my biological father's family. Unfortunately, he had passed away, but I have three half-brothers and a half-sister whom I have met and they all love me.

I married an older man who was good for me and my children. Harold and I went to visit my Canadian family last year and we had a wonderful time. Ironically, they never knew I existed until now. John, my father, had never mentioned having a child in England. But it doesn't matter — I found real happiness in Canada!

Jenny Moore (centre) surrounded by her Canadian family.

The Search for My Father
by Peter Hurricks

My name is Peter and I was born in England in March 1944. My mother, Agnes Hurricks, and my father, Jack Neale, met in 1943, when Jack was stationed near Suffolk with the Royal Canadian Engineers.

My mother was the youngest of seven children, and as all the older brothers and sisters had left home, she was expected to stay with their widowed mother. She worked for Marks and Spencer in Ipswich, and she was twenty-nine years old and still living at home when she met Jack.

I don't think my mother had a boyfriend before Jack, and in her own words she did "adore him." One of my older cousins who met him when she was a teenager said he

Jack Neale left behind wives and girlfriends in Canada and England, finally settling in Australia.

was a very charming man. He was accepted by my mother's family and regularly went out for a drink with one of my uncles. He had parcels sent to Agnes's home from his mother in Canada, apparently with his own particular brand of coffee and other items that were not available in Britain during the war.

Eventually he asked my grandmother for permission to marry Agnes. My grandmother approved, but said she didn't want my mother to go off to Canada after the war. That was all right with Jack because he said he wanted to settle in England anyway. Apparently my grandmother never really trusted him, so that's the reason why she did not want my mother taken overseas. I don't think they actually did get engaged, because soon after this Jack was posted to Yorkshire and my mother found out she was pregnant.

I don't believe that Jack was ever serious about getting engaged, let alone marrying my mother. It was just a ploy to have sex. Later in my mother's pregnancy, when it began to show, my grandmother threw Agnes out of the house and she went to London to stay with a friend.

Although it may seem strange these days, an unmarried mother in 1944 was treated as a social outcast for bringing shame and disgrace on her family. There were no income-support programs as there are today. For an unmarried mother to bring up a child on her own was tough.

Many such children were adopted, and it was not unknown for parents of unmarried mothers to commit their daughters to life in a mental institution, even though they were perfectly sane.

I was born in a London hospital. My mother was a very determined woman and she intended to keep me from the start. My grandmother did relent soon after I was born, so Agnes returned home and went back to her job at Marks and Spencer.

In April 1944, my mother took Jack to the Borough Magistrate's Court in Ipswich for maintenance costs. An affiliation order was granted for Jack to pay £0.50 per week until I reached the age of sixteen, not exactly a fortune by today's standards. Apparently he did make a few payments to my mother, but Jack's solicitor wrote to inform her that Jack was returning to Canada. With obviously no conscience on his part, the payments ceased.

Peter Hurricks as a toddler with his mother Agnes. Jack Neale was her first and only love.

One thing that surfaced during the court case was that Jack was already married in Canada with two sons, but was apparently separated from his wife. It was presumed, however, that he was returning to his family in Canada.

After the war, I think my mother must have destroyed any documents relating to Jack, because when I got to the age when I was curious about my father, there were only a couple of old photographs left.

I started to look for Jack Neale about 1980, without making any headway. I soon came up against the Canadian Privacy Act — a brick wall that I was unable to get past. This act has denied many thousands of English and Dutch war children the right to information about their fathers, and it is still in force today. Even the Canadian Charter of Rights and Freedoms does not allow access to this information.

It was not until 1997 when I contacted Project Roots that things started to progress. Until that date I was unaware of this service run by Olga and Lloyd Rains. Clearly, I now wish that I had heard of them earlier and the work they were doing, since, as it turned out, it might have given me the chance to meet my father.

As it was, in August 2001 Olga provided me with a very surprising and important lead that enabled me to trace a sister living close by in England whom I have now met. My sister, Jackie, turned out to be a lovely person, and when we met she recognized my father's likeness in me. Through Jackie, I found out about my father's Australian family and now, through our Canadian brothers, David and Wallace, I have a full picture of my father's eventful life.

At the time of my birth, my father was thirty-one years old, and given the number of years that I had been unsuccessfully trying to locate him, there was always the chance that he had not survived. This indeed turned out to be the case. He died in 1992, aged seventy-nine, in Scarborough Hospital, Yorkshire, of heart disease. His body was cremated and his ashes scattered.

Although Jack always told my mother that it was his intention to settle in England after the war, it was a great surprise to learn how much of his life he did actually spend in England, totally unknown to me.

Jack was born John Wallace Eastwood Neale in North Vancouver on February 3, 1913, the son of Annie and Wallace Neale, emigrants from Yorkshire. Jack's father was a plumber with his own business, and in the 1920s the family moved to Calgary.

In 1934, Jack married Hazel Ford in Calgary. Their first son, Wallace (named after Jack's father) was born that year. At the time, Jack was a tradesman, like his father, but it was the Depression and there was little work in Canada. To get people out of the cities, the Canadian government opened up land for homesteading, and Jack and his wife were allocated 140 acres and ten dollars a month.

The land was twenty-three miles from Rocky Mountain House in Alberta. It was a hardscrabble existence: they cleared the land and built a log house, three miles to the nearest store and twenty-three miles to the nearest doctor. Their second son, David, was born in 1938.

When World War II came, it was a way out for Jack to enlist in the Royal Canadian Engineers and an opportunity to finally get some money. Jack sent money home for a while, but in 1939 he was posted to England, the money stopped, and he left his family without means of support and never contacted them again.

The family he left behind endured considerable hardship, his wife left out in the bush with two young children in the severe winter and illness to contend with. Eventually they had to move back to Calgary and stay with Hazel's mother.

It is not known when Jack actually arrived in England in 1939, but like most Canadian servicemen during the war he was stationed on the south coast. This was where he met Nellie Godbold. On October 3, 1942, a son, Stephen, was born of this relationship. A few months later, in the early part of 1943, Jack was stationed somewhere in the Ipswich area, where he met my mother, and on March 4, 1944, I was born.

Later in 1944 my mother was informed by Jack's solicitor that Jack was returning to Canada and that she would not be able to legally claim any further support for me. But if Jack did go back to Canada, he soon returned to England because he married Stephen's mother at Brighton Registry Office on December 23, 1944. On the marriage certificate, Jack's occupation was described as Sergeant M5030 in the RCE. Four months later, in April 1945, their second child, a daughter named Jackie, was born.

The family lived in Brighton and, with a partner, Jack started a motorcycle-courier business after he left the RCE. Quite commonplace today, in the late 1940s a courier business was unique and innovative and, as it turned out, quite successful.

But as the reader might judge up until now, Jack was not well known for family commitment and responsibilities; he liked to move on. Sure enough, in the early 1950s when Australia was encouraging immigration with cheap assisted passages, Jack left his family in Brighton with the aim of a new life in Australia. He promised that when he had his feet on the ground he would send for them.

Jack being Jack, he met a woman on board ship and they started a relationship, even though she was with her husband. When they arrived in Australia they set up house together.

Jack certainly got the new life he wanted, but he forgot about the family he had deserted back in Brighton. Bearing in mind that in those days there were no social or welfare programs like today, life was very tough for Stephen, Jackie and their mother. With no income from Jack, the family was reduced to living, eating and sleeping in a single room. I thought my mother and I had difficulties at times, but they were nothing in comparison to Jackie's family. The experience of being deserted by his father apparently affected Stephen the most and was difficult for him to bear.

Meanwhile, Jack had settled in Australia and set up home with his new partner, although his wife Nellie in Brighton did not divorce him until 1967. He and his partner had a son, Robert. Surprisingly, the family stayed together for some twenty years before his Australian wife died of cancer in the mid-1970s. It is typical of Jack's lack of concern for others that, during the last two weeks of her life when she was in a hospice, he never visited once.

Although Robert had lived with his father for a long time, Jack had never talked about his past, so Robert was totally unaware of his father's Canadian family or me in England. Stephen, in the meantime, couldn't settle and decided to go to Australia to see if he could join up with his father, but apparently it didn't work out; they just didn't hit it off together.

After Jack's wife died in Australia, he asked his English ex-wife, Nellie, to re-marry him. He was now in his sixties and probably looking for companionship in his old age, and being Jack, thinking of himself again. Despite reservations from her family, Nellie remarried Jack in January 1977, in Busselton, Western Australia. In 1984, they returned to England and lived in North Yorkshire until his death in 1992.

Jack Neale as he appeared later in life.

I have met my sister Jackie and I would also like to meet my Canadian brothers at some stage, and indeed they would like to meet Jackie and me. My only regret is that all the time my father spent in England, knowing full well of my existence, he never once attempted to make contact. I think that says a lot about the man and his track record. On the face of it, he appears quite a selfish man, thinking mainly of himself and not at all shy about walking away from his responsibilities and the unhappiness he caused to so many others.

Tears of Torment
by Jill

My name is Jill. I was born on March 6, 1943, in a small coal-mining village in England. I was eleven years old when I found out that my real father was a Canadian soldier.

My mother was a married woman whose husband was a prisoner of war of the Japanese when she met my Canadian father. I was three years old in 1946 when my stepfather returned from the war. I will never forget his violence towards my mother, how he locked me up in cupboards and how he sexually abused me time after time when I was a child. I never understood why all this happened, and I always thought the reason he hurt us was that he had been tortured by the Japanese during the war.

I remember the first time I heard that my stepfather wasn't my real father. I was about eleven years old, and one of the girls at school said in a nasty way, "Your father isn't really your father." She said she had overheard her mother talk to others about it. I remember running home that day to tell my mother what the girl had said. She told me the girl was lying and just wanted to tease me, so I went back to school after lunch believing my mom instead.

Jill never found her Canadian father, but she has a new family in Olga and Lloyd Rains.

My grandmother was a widow who had her own home, and she had to work to keep everything going. She would never get involved in any disputes or arguments between my parents. Grandmother was very frightened of my stepfather and his violence. Her house was like a refuge for both my mom and me, so whenever I could, I stayed with her. I loved my grandmother a lot. She was my best friend.

As I got older I wanted to ask my grandmother about my real dad, but I never did. Without her, I would not have existed. She took me away from my brutal stepfather, and I was afraid to hurt her by bringing up the past. I suppose my mom did love me in her own way, but she always put my stepfather first. I always felt that it was guilt over my birth. But the truth is that my mother was beaten up so often she was scared to death of him. It was a matter of survival for her.

I never felt any hate towards my mother. She suffered enough. But what I couldn't forgive was that she wouldn't tell me the name of my Canadian father. My mom passed away without telling me anything at all. I don't even know if she knew his name. It is a torment I have to live with for the rest of my life.

Even after I was married and had two children, I thought she might have some respect for me and tell me something about the man who fathered me, but nothing at all. No one in the family would tell me anything about my Canadian father, so for ten long years I never saw my mother. The last time we spoke by phone, she said she didn't want to know me.

At that time I needed her so badly because my own marriage was not good and I was trying to hold my family together. My grandmother had passed away — the only one who had understood me and given me the love I needed. My marriage ended and my life became pure hell. I longed for a father and often wondered if he had only known how I suffered, would he care?

During those ten years I always said that as long as I lived I would never let my mother in my house again. Then one day the doorbell rang, and there stood my mom and my younger sister, whom I hadn't seen for years because she lived in another part of England. Mom and I looked at each other and I felt so sorry for her. She looked so old and sickly. I forgave her for all the hurt she caused me. I decided that I would try and make the best of things and stay in touch with my mom. This was very short-lived, because a few weeks later she had a brain hemorrhage. I was the only one at her bedside when she died. Then I knew that my mother had taken her secret to the grave and I would never know my father's name.

Fortunately, the relationship with my sister was good because she lived closer to me now; we became very close and were able to laugh together, which made me so happy. This was also short-lived. A few years after my mother died, my sister died at the age of fifty-three.

I placed ads in different papers in the area where my mother lived at the time I was conceived. I wanted to find someone who knew my mom at that time and see whether they could shed some light on my Canadian father. I did get some letters and phone calls, and they were mostly the same — people who had known my mother and who said she went out a lot with Canadian soldiers at the time my stepfather was a prisoner of war. They also told me that my mother had had to take me to my grandmother's house for safety after her husband came back from Japan.

The best thing to come out of the search for my father is contacting Project Roots. I would like to pay a tribute to Olga and Lloyd Rains, better known as my "Canadian mom and dad." I am their "English daughter" and I am very proud to know them. Whilst they couldn't find my father, they have written to me now for several years, and through their caring and support have been my pillar of strength.

I know that without Project Roots, and a great deal of compassion from Olga and Lloyd, many people would have never found their fathers in Canada. I will always be grateful for the happiness brought into my life by these two wonderful people. Olga and Lloyd could not find my happiness, but they have helped my hurt. They have given my life a meaning and I am proud of my Canadian mom and dad.

Scarred for the Rest of Her Life!
by Mary K.

This story is about my mother. I will call her Rosie (not her real name). My mother was seventeen years old in 1943 when the she met a young Canadian soldier in London, England. She and the soldier fell in love and dated for about a year. They planned to get married after the war's end.

Just before her boyfriend was sent to the fighting lines in Italy, Rosie knew she was pregnant. Rosie was raised in a Catholic family and had a very strict upbringing. Her parents were furious that their only daughter was pregnant by a Canadian soldier, so they were going to make her pay for bringing such shame onto the family.

They made a plan, and Rosie had to obey. She was sent to a home for unwed mothers until her son, Jimmy, was born in February 1945. Rosie was forced to sign papers turning Jimmy over to her parents. Two weeks later, Rosie slipped out of sight. For sixteen years she had no contact with her family. The shame and humiliation was too great.

At first, Rosie's parents were frantic and walked the streets of London night after night praying to find her, but they never did. For all intents and purposes, Rosie had disappeared off the face of the earth.

Some years later, Rosie married my father and had three more children, my two brothers and me. It was my dad who persuaded Rosie to look for the son she had left behind with her parents.

By the time she made contact, my grandmother had already passed away. My half-brother Jimmy, then sixteen years old, wanted nothing to do with our mother. My grandfather was still alive, and he told Rosie that her Canadian soldier had been back to see her in the hope of marriage. They had sent the young man away without telling him he had a son.

When my mother told her story to the three of us, we realized how she must have suffered when she was young and later, as a mother of three more children. She must have always thought of the baby she left behind with her parents. I asked her if she was mad at the Canadian. She said she wasn't. He had been her first love.

My mother died young. Her life was completely destroyed by this event. It scarred her for the rest of her life.

He Just Would Not Admit He Was My Dad
by Pat K.

Dear Olga and Lloyd,

Thank you so much for returning my photograph. I am sorry to tell you that I am no longer in contact with my father. He just would not admit that he was my dad. He did send me a couple of photographs of himself, also quite a nice letter, but he just kept saying he has doubts because he wasn't told about my mother's pregnancy while she was four months pregnant. He said he felt if he was responsible then he should have been told first.

When I read that, I felt I just had to explain things to him, so I phoned him that very evening to tell him my mother always had a medical condition that meant she never knew of a pregnancy until she was four or five months pregnant. Well, the minute I tried to explain this he got so mad, he said that I was pushing him and he wasn't going to have that. Just think: after fifty years he felt he was being pushed!

Anyway, he then repeated what he said the first time I called him: "What do you think you are going to get out of all this?" Before I could answer, he said, "Because I sure as hell know there's nothing in it for me."

I was so hurt and told him that I just wanted to know something about him. He said he just could not see any point in any of it and didn't want to carry on with it. I was rather upset, so I just said that I understood and said goodbye.

I waited a few days, then wrote to him explaining properly on paper about my mother's condition. I said as far as I was concerned he was, always had been and always would be my father.

My mother was not a liar. She had no reason to bring me up telling me he was my father if he was not.

To date I have never heard from him again and now sadly accept the fact that I never will. It is so sad that after all the work Project Roots did making many phone calls, writing letters, talking to so many people to find him. He did not understand your part in of all this and often told me that he did not want to hear from Project Roots anymore.

I really haven't learned anything about him at all. He would not open up to me. I sent him two photos of my two sons and me.

I feel very sad and disappointed that it ended this way. How very easy it is for a man to say that he has doubts and there is not a thing one can do about it.

At least now I expect he thinks of me, even if not exactly warmly. I would have liked so much to meet him one time and for him to see me. I suppose for that to happen would have "rocked his boat."

I really did not want anything from him at all.

I will always be grateful for all your time and effort in tracing him. I feel sad for you as well as for myself.

I wish you and Lloyd much success and hope you have more stories with happier endings than mine.

Thank you both for your kindness and bless you both.

Love, Pat K.

Devil's Brigade
by Carol Anne Hobbs

My name is Carol Anne Hobbs. I contacted Project Roots in February 2002, in search of my Canadian father, Clarence William Thompson.

I was born October 6, 1943, as the result of my mother's affair with my father, who was a Canadian soldier stationed near Croydon, Surrey, during the war. He was aware of my birth whilst serving in Italy. My mother found out he was married with children and never heard from him again.

I had been led to believe that he was killed in Italy during the war and therefore saw no reason to try to find him. During a conversation with my mother at the end of 2001, when I had mentioned how difficult it was not knowing what my father looked like or much about him, she said that she did not know for certain that he had been killed.

When I heard this, I decided to see if I could trace him. I wrote to the National Archives of Canada with his name and regiment, asking for information. At the same time, I wrote to Project Roots with my story. They put my story on the website and I waited!

I received a letter from National Archives at the beginning of April 2002, telling me he had died at Sherbrooke, Quebec, on January 13, 1995. That was all the information they could provide me with due to the Canadian Privacy Act. I was devastated to think he had died not that long ago, and thought there was no way I would be able to proceed any further. I informed Lloyd and Olga Rains, who told me to be patient ... and I waited!

C.W. Thompson in a wartime photo. His English girlfriend didn't know he was married with children in Canada.

On May 13, 2002, I received an e-mail from Olga and Lloyd saying, "We have found your Canadian family." They had spoken to Lois, the wife of my half-brother Ralph, who said they were surprised but delighted with the news and would love to make contact.

I e-mailed them immediately and we frantically exchanged correspondence. They answered all my questions and sent me photographs of Dad when he was young and through all the stages of his life. I learned that I had five brothers and three sisters. Robert (Ralph's twin) unfortunately is dead, as is Dad's wife. My three half-sisters and two half-brothers did not receive the news so well and do not want any contact with me. That, of course, is their choice. I quickly built up a great connection with my newfound brother and sister-in-law, learning all about them and their family. We spoke on the telephone, which was really exciting, and my husband suggested we go visit them in Comox, on Vancouver Island.

We flew to British Columbia on October 7, 2002, stayed in Vancouver for two days and then set off to meet my brother Ralph and his wife Lois for the first time. We were due to meet with them in Nanaimo, where they had said they would pick us up. I was feeling so excited and nervous that I was almost sick. As we walked up the ferry stairs to start the crossing over to the Island I heard my name called. Ralph and Lois were there on the ferry!

It was a wonderful moment. Apparently, Ralph could not wait any longer to meet us. We had the most lovely visit with them for five days. We were introduced to their five children and friends, and then they took us off to see some of the Island. They were so welcoming and could not do enough for us. I have enclosed a photo.

I am so grateful to Project Roots for making all this possible. I could not have found these wonderful people without them. I am only sorry I did not get to meet my father, but our children and I have, at last, got to know our Canadian roots.

My heartfelt thanks to you all once again.

With a Deeper Meaning
by Ralph Thompson

Three years ago, on the eve of the first Remembrance Day since 9/11, my family participated in the candlelight service at the cenotaph in Comox, British Columbia. We were profoundly feeling the new meaning of what our veterans, including my dad, did for us during the war — to fight, kill and die for our freedom — and what our servicemen were presently doing. Before September 11, did we ever really understand what that freedom meant?

I have always been very proud of my dad's service in the Canadian Forces and specifically in the Devil's Brigade, First Special Services Force. It has been difficult to see the passing of so many of his comrades — and finally him, in January 1995.

On Mother's Day 2002, I received a message on my answering machine from a lady in the Netherlands: "If you are the son of the late Clarence William Thompson, you have a sister in England who is looking for you."

This was a surprise —to say the least — that was not received well by the majority of my siblings, though I was pleased with the discovery of this connection to my father. The next day the call was returned, and the lady, Olga Rains of Project Roots, told us more about Carol (my father's English war child) and how to contact her.

Carol and her brother Ralph at their first meeting on the ferry to Vancouver Island, October, 2002.

The following day an e-mail arrived from my sister Carol; many e-mails and photos were exchanged, followed by emotional phone calls and then the physical contact on the Thursday of Thanksgiving weekend: October 10, 2002.

My wife, Lois, and I surprised Carol and her husband, Dave, on the B.C. ferry. We spent the next two hours getting acquainted and remarking on how she has such a Thompson resemblance. We spent the next five days looking at old photos, sharing information and then touring some of Vancouver Island.

A comfortable kinship developed very quickly with Carol as well as Dave. She is truly a delightful person, and I proudly call her my sister. Dave told me when I first talked to him on the phone that I had a wonderful sister. Turns out her husband is an amazingly devoted husband and a kind, caring person as well. They are a wonderful couple. My only regret of our uniting is that she never got to meet, touch or hug our dad.

The saying goes that there is always good that comes out of bad. The war and its awful carnage had a side that I had not thought about much, and that was male-female relationships. Out of those relationships, an estimated 30,000 babies with Canadian fathers were conceived, and my sister was one of them.

Many have never found their roots, and there is a wonderful service committed to helping people find their kin. It is the Project Roots website. It is an amazing website that is the reality of incomplete lives of people who simply wish to know their roots. Thirty thousand wonderful Canadian human beings are the byproduct of World War II.

It is my greatest hope that this letter will provide the avenue for at least one father and adult child to experience the meeting, touch and hug, as many have been unable to share that cherished moment due to the fact that many aging veterans have already passed on.

I equally hope that many siblings can find each other and experience the joy that Carol and I now have added to our lives. As this Remembrance Day approaches, my wife, children and I have a new found depth of understanding, and "we will remember them," including Dad (Grandpa), with our deepest respect and honour, as always. We will also remember their war-born children with empathy, respect and honour.

Remembering — The War Within
by Karen Cockwell

As Remembrance Day approaches, I know that I will once again stand at the local cenotaph in the cold, damp November air, my eyes glistening with tears as I listen to the brass band playing "Abide with Me."

I shall not mourn, however, for the fresh-faced young soldiers who now lay buried in graves so far from home; nor will I mourn for those smartly dressed sailors who are buried at sea. Neither will I mourn for those intrepid airmen who flew combat missions over enemy territory and went down in flames.

These servicemen already have thousands of people who remember their passing every year. Their graves are attended by the grateful nations who honour them for their ultimate sacrifice.

Rather, as I have done for all my life, I shall shed my tears for a man who served his country overseas for five and a half years in the Second World War and survived. He returned home and lived for another fifty-three years.

What could possibly be the quality of life for a person who had spent his youth watching others die in the most horrible way? How would he deal with the knowledge that he had contributed to their slaughter? Why would I, his daughter, mourn for a man who did not die? Let me explain.

He was a twenty-one-year-old youth — tall, well-built, with a thatch of dark curly hair and piercing blue eyes. He had a slightly crooked smile and a small vertical scar on his chin acquired during one of his many amateur boxing matches. Long hours of work on his grandparents' farm during the Depression had honed his muscles into fine form.

By the summer of 1939 he was working as a moulder in a foundry. He was a handsome charmer who had his pick of many young ladies and had fallen in love with a raven-haired, freckle-faced young lady almost three years his senior.

He loved excitement, so when war was declared on September 1, he immediately signed up with little regard for his ailing mother or his lady love. Within days he was off to basic training in Brantford, Ontario. Two weeks later he came home to a hastily arranged marriage to his sweetheart. He made one more trip back home in December before heading to England on the *Empress of Britain*.

What happened to him next has been the subject of much speculation by my family. Although I have sent for his war records, the Department of Veterans Affairs has not replied. We do know, however, that he spent the first part of the war in England and Scotland. We also know that he fell in love with a Scottish girl with whom he fathered two children.

We have snapshots of him sitting proudly on his motorcycle as a dispatch rider. His letters to his wife say little about his service, although they contain numerous complaints about the tobacco pool and cigarettes that were sent to him that he did not receive. One telegram even requests a change of brands — to Buckinghams!

The best record that we can find concerning his service is contained in several newspaper clippings which we found tucked into the old family Bible. According to these reports he took part in the battles of Ortona, Gustof Line, Hitler Line before the fall of Rome, and the battle of the Gothic Line. These were all severe campaigns that left him suffering from battle fatigue. He was wounded in Sicily and his life was saved by an Italian woman named Carmelita. Little wonder, then, that he smoked! Unfortunately his smoking led to a lifelong struggle with lung disease that eventually claimed his life. More devastating to his family was a dependency on alcohol which he was never able to completely overcome, and he became a master of subterfuge, keeping his wife guessing where his booze was hidden. We will never know how much the war contributed to this addiction, but we suspect it was a great deal.

He came home a veteran — at the ripe old age of twenty-six! — of the most horrible scenarios that life has to offer. His discharge papers say that he was unable to meet the required military physical standards. The war ended several months later, but his private war lasted for the rest of his life. His discharge papers do not tell us just how unfit he was. They do not tell us that he would rise up in bed in the middle of the night, screaming with nightmares. They do not tell us that his nerves were so bad that he would lash out in anger at anything that displeased him. They do not tell us that he was so short-tempered that his five-year-old daughter, who had prayed for his safe return ever since she was old enough to walk, was terrified of him and never recovered from that fear.

Neither do they tell us that he might become physically abusive to those he loved the most. They do not tell us about the mental anguish that tortured him as he tried to decide, prior to his return to Canada, if he should stay with his "wife" and children in Scotland or come home to the wife he had never actually lived with and the daughter he had never seen.

Since the army had a policy of sending soldiers home to work out their own destinies, he returned to Canada and buried his memories of that other life and that other family. They were never spoken of again.

Almost all recollections of those five years were pushed into a part of his memory from which they were never allowed to emerge. Only the portrait of him in his first uniform, the waves of his brown hair softly curling around his peaked cap, the gilded frame proudly proclaiming "For King and Country," remained hanging on the living room wall.

On the rare occasion when he hosted a party at his house, he could be heard belting out a few of the old army songs. I never really understood some of the words, but "Roll Me Over, Lay Me Down and Do It Again" seemed self-evident. Buried with the memories was a letter from King George VI thanking him for being in the first contingent to join up.

Aside from the portrait and the songs, there was one time each year when he allowed his memories to surface. Each year on Remembrance Day, his wife would polish up his five medals, which hung from five brightly-striped ribbons. With them proudly displayed on the jacket of his blue-serge police uniform, he would march with head held high to the cenotaph. Was it this resurgence of memories that led him to the inevitable drinking bout that followed?

His last parade was the one that he observed from the window of the hospital solarium as he sat in his wheelchair beside his ailing wife of fifty-seven years. The once-sparkling blue eyes had become rheumy and the tall, strong frame had become wasted with Parkinson's disease. He no longer smoked, but the damage had been done long before. He seldom drank — it was too hard to get to the bottle. His nerves had calmed down somewhat, but he railed long and loud at the Parkinson's before it finally robbed him of his voice.

His body was covered with a rash of undetermined origin. As he neared death, no amount of either subtle or overt prompting could unleash the memories buried so deep in his psyche. There had never been any healing of those combat-induced nightmares, the bad nerves that plagued him for years or the addictions that caused his death. Time has caused the memories to fade, like his old uniform, to remain locked away forever.

So, once again this Remembrance Day, I shall weep for my father. My tears will flow for all those soldiers who fought "for King and country" and came home to a life of frustration, trauma and anger. Only when my father lay dying did I perceive his strength. When he needed me, I learned to love him. When he died, I forgave him. Yes, on November 11, I shall remember and I shall mourn.

I Found My Roots in Canada
by Maureen Fletcher

Maureen Fletcher's father, Bill, lived in Nova Scotia after the war.

Project Roots found my father, Bill, through one of his relatives, and through them I was introduced to my aunts and cousins in Toronto. I have been to Canada to meet my father's family, and except for one of his sisters, they have all accepted me unconditionally as a member of the family.

While it is touching to be so embraced by strangers, it is clear that this side of my father's family did not know him very well; he travelled all over the world with his work and eventually settled in Nova Scotia. But there was someone else who knew my father: a woman named Helen in Nova Scotia, to whom I was introduced.

After a glorious visit with the Toronto family, I went to Nova Scotia to visit Helen and her family. Helen had been good friends with my father (she was not his girlfriend) and she was able to tell me more about him.

My father was never married, and before he passed away he gave his medals to Helen, and she in turn passed them on to me. Receiving these was a very emotional experience, and as a result I wrote a poem about it, which appears on page 65.

I could not have been prepared for the emotions I felt knowing my father had chosen to live in such a lovely place. The beauty and serenity touched my heart. Having learned from Helen and her family about his personality, his interest in music, art and reading, I believe he was a man of some depth whom I would have liked very much.

Temperamentally I was not like my mother, and I often wondered if I might take after my father. So it gave me a big thrill when many of Helen's family said how much I looked like him. As I am writing now, a big lump comes into my throat because it really does mean so much to me.

My five days with Helen and her family in Nova Scotia were spent driving around to see the various projects my father had been involved with as a construction engineer. One of Helen's daughters lived in the house my father had built, so I have been in my father's house!

They took me to the hospital in Glace Bay where my father died. Although some people might think that was morbid, I was touched that they had put so much thought into making this trip have meaning for me.

I have often thought that if things had been different and my mother had married Bill, I would not have had the lovely family I did. In the long run, I now feel that I have the best of everything — I grew up with two lovely half-sisters and a half-brother. Now I also have discovered my father, giving me knowledge of my roots and an insight to my identity. To make things better, I have also gained a new Canadian family and friendships. It's perfect.

Maureen Fletcher (right) with her Canadian family.

Losses
by Maureen Fletcher

Dear Bill,

When you gazed at these medals, what did you see
Two stars and three circles, what did they mean?

Do you think of the glory or the terror of war
Of a comrade who had gone and no more would you know
Did you think of white crosses all dappled with sun
Of all of those losses and a brother so young
Did you think of a love you had found and then lost
Of the price that was paid and the terrible cost
Did you think of a baby so sweet and so small
Of the daughter you lost when you answered the call

When you gazed at these medals, what did you see
Two stars and three circles, what did they mean?

When I gaze at these medals, what do I see
Two stars and three circles, what do they mean?
 I think of a soldier so handsome and tall
Of a smile so engaging as he answered that call
I think of his mother waiting at home
Of the three sons who left her, and just two to return
I think of my mother, who loved him the most
Of the love that she found and the love that she lost
I was that baby so sweet and so small
I am the daughter so proud of a father not known

When I gaze at these medals, what do I see
Two stars and three circles, what do they mean?

With love,
Your daughter, Maureen

The Liberation of Holland
by Olga Rains

"I know, because I was there."

Partying went on for weeks after the Liberation of Holland. In this photo, happy Dutch citizens crowd a Jeep filled with liberators of the Princess Patricia's Canadian Light Infantry.

When the war was over in Holland, and the liberators joined the liberated, they celebrated! That summer is remembered as "The Wild Summer of 1945," and I know, because I was there.

One has to understand the situation in Holland at the time. The war had been very hard on the civilian population, especially that last winter when we were cut off by Allied advances elsewhere. The winter of 1944–45 was unusually severe. Called "The Hunger Winter," it was marked by extreme fuel and food shortages. Dutch citizens ate tulip bulbs and dirt to survive. People died of starvation in the streets.

After five brutal years of war, the normal standards of social behaviour had shifted somewhat, changing women's and men's roles and undermining traditional notions of right and wrong in families. Parental authority was undermined and challenged by independence-seeking daughters. Fathers and brothers, who would normally have exerted pressure on the young women to behave, had either been taken away long ago as slave labour or were in hiding. Into this vacuum young Dutch women were given positions of unusual responsibility. Even teenaged girls became their family's sole support, walking hours to a farmer's field for a bit of food to keep their family alive.

By May 1945, the population was at its physical and psychological breaking point. Then, suddenly, Holland was free once more and as the liberators entered our country, we were overjoyed.

Only those who were there will understand those emotional times. We were so glad to have survived the war. The Dutch people were still alive. The soldiers were alive. Is it any wonder that everybody was overjoyed? The Dutch, a reticent race of people, welcomed these heroes with open arms. There was dancing and romancing all over the country, and by June there were an estimated 170,000 Canadian soldiers in Holland. At dance-hall parties organized by Canadian regiments and units, the soldiers and civilian women mixed, dancing and partying into the wee hours of the morning.

It was inevitable that Dutch women would become pregnant by the Canadians. Before too long, the numbers of young pregnant Dutch women climbed into the hundreds and thousands. Clerics and municipal officials began to speak out against the social problem caused by the illegitimate births of half-Canadian children. Disapproving articles began to appear in the press. The Canadian government responded by saying it assumed no responsibility for illegitimate children and would not compel the fathers to do so.

Meantime, the repatriation of these Canadian soldiers was slow, because there was a shortage of transatlantic shipping. By August 1945, only 60,000 soldiers had departed for home. By the time the last Canadian soldiers finally departed for Canada in 1946, they left behind a lasting and bitter legacy of thousands of half-Canadian children.

To be honest, many of the soldiers didn't know they had left a pregnant girlfriend behind. But many others did.

Marriages were discouraged by both Dutch and Canadian parents, as well as the Canadian Army. It was not always with selfish attitudes, but with thought for the well-being of both the Dutch girl and the returning soldier. The soldier and the girl came from two different worlds, with different ways and cultures.

What about the baby who was to come? Nobody gave much thought to them because they weren't even born yet. But more than 7,000 illegitimate births were recorded in the Netherlands in 1946, compared with 2,500 in 1939.

Some of the mothers married just to give their baby a name, not realizing that it would have been better for her and the baby had she stayed single. There were mothers who did stay single because they worried about their children being abused by stepfathers. When a mother married, the child immediately received the father's name. Until then, the child had the mother's maiden name.

These young Dutch mothers — in many cases, heartbroken or very sick — encountered a lot of interference from their families. In those days it was shameful to have a baby out of wedlock, and many parents tried to hide the secret from their families, friends and neighbours. In the southern part of Holland, the church's influence was pervasive, and there is no telling how much heartbreak they caused. Babies were taken away from their mothers against their will.

All that some of these half-Canadian youngsters remember is living in "homes." Some were moved from one "home" to another. When they started school and the teacher or the other children found out that they had a Canadian father, fingers would be pointed at them. They were different, they were half-Canadian, and they were not accepted.

These youngsters were called names. Often, when things got too bad, the family would move. Many Dutch war children refer to their childhood as a time of being moved from home to home, or being passed from one aunt to another aunt. They were the so-called "family possessions," because they had no fathers.

Most of the Liberation children had a difficult childhood because they somehow felt different. At home they were the eldest in the family and had to do many chores. Their relationships with their Dutch fathers was not always good, and in many cases the mothers suffered also, because anger was taken out on the Canadian children.

The Dutch grandparents played a big role in the lives of the Liberation children; in fact, many were raised by their *opa* or *oma*. The mothers, most of them young girls, had to go out and work to support the child. There was no help available from either the Dutch or Canadian governments. Unlike today, there was no welfare, so the mother had the responsibility of raising the child. The pressure under which they had to live was sometimes too much to bear, and some died young, leaving their fatherless babies behind.

In Holland, as in Britain and elsewhere, Canadian fathers have tended not to come looking for their war children. Those who have are few and far between. Most of them knew all along that they had left behind a baby in Holland, but they married their old sweethearts and started a new life in postwar Canada. Others were racked with guilt, which led to an inner turmoil that affected their lives and Canadian families. Many have since died, but for those who have been reunited with their Dutch offspring, there is great joy and relief that their wartime secret is finally out in the open for all to see.

Preparing to leave for Canada, a soldier says goodbye to his Dutch friends. Left to right: Frieda Trestorff, Leslie Rains, Olga Rains (nee Trestorff), Sophia Trestorff and Augusta van der Vliet (a Canadian cousin).

I Met My First Love after the Liberation
by Mira

My name is Mira and I live in Nijmegen, Holland. I met my first love after the Liberation, at a dance organized by the Canadians. I will never forget those times as long as I live.

Louis was a French-Canadian and he was very good-looking. He worked in the kitchen in the big armouries just outside the city. We spent as much time together as we could, and one day I brought him home to meet my parents. The first thing they asked him about was his religion. Like us, Louis was Catholic, so we clicked right away.

During the winter of 1944–45 we had a wonderful time together. We went dancing and spent a lot of time at the kitchen where he worked. We were so in love and we started talking about marriage after the war was over.

As time went on, Louis was getting a bit impatient. He wanted to be alone with me and for us to go to bed together, but I was still a virgin and I knew nothing about sex. About the same time, I found a note from my mother in my coat pocket. She wrote, "I have noticed the way that Louis is looking at you, and the way he touches you. I am sure you know what I mean and what I am talking about. This is a warning for you. If you become pregnant, don't come home anymore."

I was eighteen years old, but I was green as grass and I needed to be informed about sex. I went to my mother that same evening and asked her to tell me about the birds and the bees. Her face turned red and she walked away from me. Whom else could I ask? The priest? He would probably think that I already had sinned and call my parents.

I was very upset, and Louis tried to comfort me. He took me in his arms and I broke down and told him the story. He just laughed and called me his "little virgin." He pulled a small box with white tablets out of his pocket. He told me that if I took one of these before having sex I would not get pregnant.

Louis knew how stupid and innocent I was. I wanted to believe him because I was so afraid of losing him. That night, we had sex for the first time. When I arrived home, I could not look my parents in the face.

A few months later, I still was not pregnant, so I began to believe it was those little white pills that the Canadian boys were issued. But as time went on, sure enough I did become pregnant. I kept it to myself for a while to be absolutely certain, and the first person I told was Louis. I will never forget that day. He told me that he was already married in Canada. He would tell his wife, that's all. No more.

I asked him to come home with me and tell my parents. He told them it was all his fault and that he was sorry. They asked him to leave at once.

I missed Louis so much, but my parents prevented me from going out, so I could not leave the house to see him. I heard later that he came to the door but was refused entry.

My parents decided that I could stay home for the first few months, but after that I was to go to a home for unwed mothers who had Canadian babies. I soon found out that I wasn't the only one taken for a sex ride by a Canadian soldier.

My mother had decided that they would take the baby and raise it like my brother or sister. I had to sign papers after the birth signing all my rights over to my parents.

I so hoped that Louis would come back for me, but he never did. Once, he sent his friend with an envelope containing 400 guilders and a message that he would contact me after the war.

My world had fallen apart. I had turned from a happy young girl into a serious young woman with a very big problem.

In the home, pregnant girls had to pay for their sins and were made to do all the impossible and ugly tasks. There was no love or compassion there. I could write much more, but I am ashamed to say how I suffered at the hands of my own people. The day I went into labour, I had to scrub the wooden floors in the hall.

I had a terrible time when Sonja was born, but she was so beautiful and perfect. They promised to let me hold her if I signed the papers, so I did. I knew I couldn't win. I held her small warm body to my breasts. She was the only baby I ever had.

Sonja grew up; we all loved her. She had the dark eyes from Louis and my blonde hair. She was a beauty. Sonja knew me as her older sister, and there were two brothers in between us.

It wasn't until my parents died that Sonja came to me and revealed that she had known that I was her mother since she was sixteen years old. One of the older members of our family had told her secretly about her father and me.

Sonja and I are lucky. We always had a good relationship as sisters, and now it is even better because I can be her mother. Together we decided to find her father so she could meet him. Knowing that he had been married, we had to be very careful. The people who helped us were very discreet. Louis's family was found. He had passed away ten years earlier, but his large family in Canada was interested in meeting her. Sonja and I cried together. Apparently, the family knew that Louis had left a child in Holland. On his deathbed he confessed, but they didn't have a name.

Postscript: Sonja and Mira visited Louis's family in Canada a few years ago. Louis and his wife had twelve children who accepted their half-sister with open arms. Louis's wife and Mira are good friends and they visit each other yearly.

In this photo, Dutch civilians celebrate Liberation by crowding on a Jeep of the 1st Canadian Corps. May 10, 1945. Dean, Michael M. / Canada. Dept. of National Defence / Library and Archives Canada.

Irene Means Peace
by Olga Rains

Katja was a young woman from Apeldoorn who met her Canadian soldier, Bill, in the summer of 1945. By the time Katja realized she was pregnant in November, Bill was already repatriated to Canada and it took her a long time to accept that he was never coming back.

Six months into the pregnancy, she was confronted by her mother and was immediately shuffled off to a private home for unwed mothers in Amsterdam. On July 7, 1946, the baby was born and Katja named her Irene (Dutch for "peace").

Irene was taken away by Katja's parents and raised by them as their child. Katja's pain at never being allowed to raise her daughter and her guilt over the shame of having a baby out of wedlock were personal torments her entire life.

In 1986, Katja heard Lloyd and Olga Rains on a radio show about the war children born in Holland. She immediately wrote to the Rains and in a series of letters told them her life story. Katja has since died, and what follows is her story based on her letters to Project Roots.

Katja found Olga Rains on a radio talk show in 1986 and she wrote to Olga about the search for Bill, her Canadian boyfriend. When the Rains finally found Bill, he wanted nothing to do with his Dutch war child.

Dear Olga Rains,

I heard you on the radio this morning and I want you to know that I am one of the mothers you were talking about.

My little girl was born on July 7, 1946, in Amsterdam. I named her Irene, which means peace. Yes, there was peace; the Canadian liberators had freed us from the Nazis. And there was celebration, after five long years of living under the Germans. There was much happiness.

I met Bill in Apeldoorn after the Liberation in the summer of 1945. He was a Canadian soldier stationed in the area where I lived. We fell in love and were inseparable. A few weeks after we met, Bill moved to Hilversum, further away from my family's home in Apeldoorn. Despite the distance, he still came to see me every chance he had. Often I would go with him and stay overnight in a room in a private home in return for cigarettes and soap.

We went out together to shows and dancing, and life was so wonderful then after the dark years of war. We made plans to get married, and Bill was going to ask my father for my hand.

That same night, we went to bed together for the first time!

A few weeks later, Bill came with the bad news that his regiment was going back to Canada. He tried to stay and get a transfer to another regiment, but it was not possible. He had to leave. He promised to come back and marry me or he would send me the fare to come to Canada.

Our last night together, we were sad and heavy-hearted. I will never forget how we both cried as the truck slowly pulled out of the schoolyard. Sad, yes, but at least I was still full of hope that we would be together some day.

A few weeks later, I knew that I was pregnant. I didn't tell my parents. I wrote to Bill and asked him when he was coming back. I needed him so much at that time. Even a letter would have helped to ease the pain.

All alone and with no one to talk to about my problem, I decided to have an abortion, but I had no money at all. I kept hoping that Bill would be able to send me some money. I even asked him in one of my letters, but he never answered a single one of them. Little did I know that when he drove out of the schoolyard that night in 1945, I would never see him again.

Six months pregnant and alone, I was at my wit's end. Then my mother started to suspect something, so I told her. All hell broke loose! My mother and father were outraged; it was all my fault and I had to leave home soon as possible before the family and neighbours found out.

That day, I left the house with a plan to commit suicide. I walked and walked in sort of a trance; I didn't see the people who passed me on the street. I felt as if I was going crazy. I wanted to cry, but I couldn't. When it was getting dark, I sat down on a bench in the park close to where I lived.

Then I felt the baby move, and tears started to stream down my face. I knew then that I could not have an abortion.

My parents had been out looking for me, and when I saw their worried faces, I decided to listen to the plan they had made for me. I went to a home for unwed mothers in Amsterdam. It was a private home with about ten girls who were all expecting Canadian babies. Fortunately, the people were very good to us there. They taught us how to care for and love our babies.

But it wasn't free. I had to buy off my life insurance and I sold my cigarette and candy rations in order to pay for the privilege.

At the time, I loved to smoke, something I had learned from Bill. But I couldn't afford to smoke because I needed the money to pay the home.

The peace of the home was shattered on the night Irene was born. I had to go to the Wilhelmina Hospital in Amsterdam and the staff was hateful to women with Canadian babies. They called me dirty names and left me alone in the labour room until Irene was born. Back in the ward, I had a grey blanket made from sack cloth. When I looked around, I saw two more beds with the same blankets. Later, I found out that these were also girls who had Canadian babies. This was done on purpose, so that everybody could see that we were sinners.

My only visitors were the other women from the home. Not even my parents came to see me and their new granddaughter. For three months, I lived at the home when my mother came down to see me and the baby. Irene was beautiful, and my mother decided that I should come home with her. I was to go to work and she would look after Irene ... and that was an order.

Everybody in my family loved Irene and she got much attention. I found a job and worked long, hard hours to be able to support the child my parents had taken as their own.

Irene called my mother "Mama" and my father "Pappa," and this was very hard for me to accept.

With the help of a good friend, we made up a letter to the Canadian Department of Veterans Affairs and asked for Bill's address. An answer came back from a lawyer who said he would act as a go-between for Bill and me.

I had to borrow money to pay the lawyer, of course. I sent Bill photos of Irene, and I was sure that he would get in touch with us, but he never did.

I started dating again, and twice I had a serious relationship. The first one broke off the moment I mentioned that Irene was my baby. The second fellow wanted to marry me, but his parents did everything to stop it.

An old friend of mine I hadn't seen for years had heard of my problems. He lived in another part of Holland and called me one day to have dinner with him. He had his share of problems in his marriage. His wife had left him and he had to raise two young children with the help of a housekeeper.

We decided to give it a try. I would take Irene and look after his two children. He had a good job, so I didn't have to work anymore.

But when I proposed the idea to my parents, they told me in no uncertain terms that they wouldn't let go of Irene and there was nothing I could do about it. Irene was happy, so why upset her? I'd lost my child and I knew it.

We moved to another part of Holland, and I had another girl and a boy. I have a good husband and lovely children, but I am not happy. All my life I have felt guilty about what happened during the Liberation, and I will until I die.

Postscript: Katja died in 1988, leaving behind some letters I had written to her in 1986 about her search for Bill. In her first letter, she had asked us to find Bill; the second letter cancelled the request. She felt that Bill would not accept Irene, and she was so right.

After Katja's husband died and the house was sold, the letter I had written was found by Irene. She wrote us a letter and asked us to find Bill. We searched, without success.

Irene called one day and told us she was going to Canada for a holiday. We encouraged her to go to the Records Centre in Ottawa. They were willing to get in touch with Bill, who was still living. They wrote him a letter asking him to call the office; he didn't. They wrote a second letter, after which he called and made it very clear that he wanted nothing to do with his Dutch daughter because "it was too long ago."

The Shock Killed Him!
by Olga Rains

For years, Alma had tried to find her father, Martin Cline, a Canadian soldier who was stationed with the Winnipeg Rifles in Holland at the end of World War II.

Alma's mother, Grietje, met Martin at a liberation party in the village where she lived. Grietje's parents had a farm and she had to do her daily chores — milking cows, feeding the chickens and cleaning the barn. Martin was of Ukrainian origin, and his parents had a farm in Manitoba, so he felt right at home and came over often to help. The couple fell in love and plans were made to get married before Martin went back to Canada. The idea was that Grietje could follow him later on the war bride ships.

Victorious Canadian troops enter Amsterdam as thousands of joyous citizens gather in the streets to celebrate. The partying went on for weeks!

Following rules laid out by the Canadian Army, Martin went to his commanding officer and asked for permission to marry. Accordingly, he filled out the paperwork to get married in Holland. But before they could get married, Martin's regiment was repatriated to Canada. This was a terrible disappointment for both of them because Grietje was now pregnant.

Martin was very happy knowing that there was a baby coming. They made plans to start a small farm on the lot Martin would be able to purchase with the help of Veterans Affairs in Canada. The last week before Martin left for Canada, he came with the news that he was being shipped to England in preparation for the transatlantic crossing. To everyone's surprise, he announced that the wedding would take place in England and that he would make preparations for Grietje's journey to Canada on one of the war bride ships. The last night he was in Holland, Grietje's parents had a party for the happy couple. Martin promised to let Grietje know as soon as he knew the date of the wedding.

That was the last Grietje ever heard from Martin.

Several months after Martin left, Grietje enlisted the help of her older brother, Wim, who understood English, and wrote a letter to Martin's address in Canada. She waited and waited, but there was no answer.

In June 1946, the baby was born and a brokenhearted Grietje named her little daughter Alma, after her grandmother who had been killed during the war.

Grietje's brother decided to find out what happened to Martin. He wrote a long letter to the Canadian legation in The Hague. They wrote back and promised that they would send an inquiry to Veterans Affairs in Canada to interview Martin.

A month later the answer came:

> Mr. Martin Cline was interviewed. He denies even knowing your sister. He is now in civilian life and married and he accepts no responsibility whatsoever.
>
> I am very sorry for your sister in her misfortune and that we are unable to do anything more for her. I might refer her to the Red Cross who will assist in such cases.
>
> Yours truly
> Major H.J.C
> Canadian Legation

Alma grew up with her grandparents and her mother, Grietje, at the farm. When she was old enough, she began to ask questions. They told her all kinds of stories about her father — everything but the truth.

On her fourteenth birthday Alma had a party, and family and friends were invited. While she was playing with a cousin, she heard the big secret that had been in the family for years. Everyone knew the truth except her.

After that, Alma's relationship with her mother became very bad and, being a teenager, she rebelled and blamed her mother for everything. Grietje's health had gradually gotten worse over the years. She had worked so hard to forget what had happened after the Liberation. She never married — and it wasn't that she didn't get offers. Grietje couldn't trust another man after what Martin had done to her.

Alma was only eighteen when she married Andy. They had known each other since high school. They had two little girls, and one of them bore a striking resemblance to her grandfather, Martin Cline.

Grietje died young, when she was only thirty-nine years old. After the funeral, Alma talked to different family members, who told her what had happened when Martin left. For the first time, she heard what Grietje never wanted her to know.

It was then that Alma decided to find her roots, and the father she never knew, in Canada. She was determined to find him. It took a very long time, because he had moved from Manitoba to the other side of Canada.

When we found Martin Cline in 1998, he was surprised to say the least. At first he lied to us and said that he was the wrong person, so we had to check all our facts again to be certain. But he was the right Martin Cline — there was no doubt. Alma wrote him a nice letter asking him only about her roots. She sent him photos of herself and her two daughters, who looked even more like him as they got older.

She heard nothing for a long time. Then a very short letter arrived. It was written by Mrs. Cline, Martin's Canadian wife.

> I don't want any more letters and photos. In your letter you said you were hoping he was over the shock. You did a good job, the shock killed him and how do you think I feel now? He was my husband!

Alma wanted photos of her father, so we contacted Martin's younger brother in another part of Canada. He knew the story from way back and was reluctant to get involved, but he thought his wife might want to help, so I phoned the aunt and explained how important it was for Alma to have those photos. She promised that she would try, but it would take time, as she had to write family members who were scattered over Canada.

She did keep her promise, and a year later a big envelope arrived with photos of the whole family — all Alma's aunts and uncles and grandparents. After so many years of searching, she finally knew her Canadian roots. In the Cline family pictures, Alma could clearly see that her daughters look just like her family in Canada.

She Thought He Was Dead
by Olga Rains

Elly and Stan met just before the Liberation of Holland in the village where Elly lived near the Yssel River. Stan and his regiment were to cross that river and fight through the last occupied part of Holland. There was heavy fighting, and many young Canadian soldiers lost their lives.

Stan promised Elly that if he came out of this alive he would contact her the first chance he got. The night before the big crossing, Elly and Stan cried until there were no tears left. They spent the whole night together, just in case they would never see each other again.

Elly crawled in through her bedroom window early in the morning so her parents wouldn't know she had been out all night. She couldn't sleep for thinking about Stan. When she heard her parents, she got up at once and told them she was going towards the river, but they stopped her. The fighting was too heavy.

Like Elly and Stan in this story, many young couples met and fell in love following the Liberation. In this photo taken in the summer of 1945, Lloyd and Olga Rains (left) pose for a photo with friends.

When Elly didn't hear anything from Stan after the war ended, she presumed that he was dead. She soon found out that she was pregnant, and what was in store for her. In those days an illegitimate child was an utter shame, and a poor girl in that condition would be the talk of the village. Elly's parents were very displeased about it and treated her more like an orphan than their own child. She was kept out of the public eye and was put to work as a maid. Throughout her entire pregnancy, Elly never once saw a doctor and never left the house.

With no one to talk to and no sympathy from her parents, Elly silently endured her suffering, but it had a deep psychological impact that marked the rest of her life.

The day her baby was to be born, a neighbour who was not at all qualified was called to help with the birth. It happened in a dark room in the back of the house, without proper facilities or medical care. Elly never forgot the birth of her little boy under such circumstances. She never had any more children.

Little Ben was a cute, likeable and handsome little fellow. From the start, his grandparents spoiled him more than was good for him. Ben was like a favourite pet who could do no harm. Elly had to look for work to earn their keep.

Elly did shift work, so she'd either have to get up very early or come home very late. Some nights, when Ben was restless, Elly had to look after him and did not get the sleep she needed. She lost weight and became rundown, but her mother insisted that she get up and look after Ben at night — after all, it was her baby. Instead of love and under-standing, Elly received abuse and coldness.

Through all her misery, Elly prayed almost daily that someday Stan would return. She would dream about it and wake up crying. When Ben was almost a year old, a letter came from Canada addressed to Elly. Her mother opened it before Elly came home and read that Stan was planning to come and fetch Elly and take her to Canada. He had been wounded and had not been able to write.

When Elly arrived home that day, she heard the bad news that Stan had been killed — her mother lied to her. In the meantime, Elly's mother wrote back to Stan that Elly was married and that he should not bother her anymore. She never mentioned the baby.

Elly went out of her mind and literally hit her head against a brick wall in sheer frustration. This was too much for her; now all her hope was gone. Then she met Bert, who tried to help her; she told him her problems. He accepted little Ben, who was a very busy little boy of almost four. His behaviour was sometimes very strange: he got into mischief a lot, always wanted his own way. His grandparents couldn't handle him anymore, so when Elly and Bert got married, they took Ben far away from his grandparents.

Ben became a problem child and ended up in a reformatory when he was fifteen.

As for Elly, the biggest blow in her life came when she found out many years later that Stan had been looking for her. He had seen a documentary war children on Canadian TV. This got him thinking sbout Elly and his suspicions that her mother had lied to him so many years ago. He knew Elly's last name and called Project Roots and asked if we could find her.

We searched in and around the village where she had lived, but there was no one by that name. We had to make a lot of calls until we finally found a member of the family who told us that Elly and her husband had moved to Belgium. Unfortunately, he didn't know where. He did know her married name, but he knew nothing about a son.

More calls, and finally we had the right number. Elly answered the telephone. When I mentioned that Stan was looking for her, she started crying and screaming. I couldn't talk to her. When I called back later, her husband answered and told me what had happened after the war, that Elly was told Stan had been killed. He also said Elly had a child with Stan, a boy named Ben.

Elly was lucky to have a good and understanding husband who helped her get over the initial shock, but she really never did recover from the news that Stan was alive.

When I told Stan the whole story, he started crying. He called back later and told me about the letter, about how much he had loved Elly and wanted to marry her. Stan hoped to meet his son, so I called Elly's husband to see if that could be arranged. He and Stan corresponded, but Bert explained that Elly wasn't up to seeing him — maybe later on. This was never to be. Elly's life ended a year later. It had all been too much for her.

In 1985, Stan came to Europe and visited Elly's grave in Belgium. His plan to visit Ben was not to be, either. Ben did not want to meet his biological father. Stan passed away in 1990 in Saskatchewan.

Where Is Fred?
by Olga Rains

When we first met Johnny Bruggenkamp in 1982, he was carrying a small briefcase with all the information he had gathered about his Canadian father's regiment and the places where they had stayed during World War II. Although Johnny had a photograph, he did not know his father's last name or where he came from in Canada. All he had to go on was a picture and a name: Fred.

Johnny was one of many illegitimate children born in the town of Sneek in the Dutch province of Friesland. Sneek had the most half-Canadian babies in Holland because there were many Canadian soldiers billeted in small homes with families that were already too big for such small dwellings.

Johnny's mother was only sixteen when she got pregnant, and as soon as it became known, her Canadian soldier was promptly transferred to West Germany. That did not stop the two lovers from communicating, however. As Johnny found out later, his mother did know Fred's last name, because she wrote to him in Germany and in Alvinston, Ontario, where he returned after the war.

Johnny was raised by his grandparents and knew his mother as one of his sisters. He was an adolescent when he learned that his "parents" were really his grandparents and his "big sister" was his mother. It was a blow to the young teenager: knowing that his father had abandoned him and that his mother had given him up produced immense turmoil, and he attempted suicide.

Not a day went by when Johnny didn't think of his Canadian dad. With only a blurred photograph, Johnny spent hours and hours going from door to door to find someone who had known Fred.

He finally did find the house where Fred had stayed, but the owners were dead and the daughter was only six years old when Fred had been there. She did provide Johnny with a better photograph of his father. Written on the back of the photo was one word: Fred. There was no last name.

When we met Johnny, he was so happy that we would try to help him find his Canadian roots. We were in touch with the regiment Fred had served with, but they could not — or would not — help.

In 1983, Lloyd and I made a trip across Canada to find some of these missing Canadian fathers. We did not know where in Canada Fred was from. Even the publicity gained through newspapers and TV programs where Fred's photo was shown was not successful.

Later, we heard that one of his sons lived in Calgary. We had spent a few days in Calgary during that 1983 tour and were on TV and radio and in the newspaper, me holding Fred's photo, but Fred's son did not see the story.

It wasn't until years later, in November, 1987, when we were house-sitting in Lambeth, a village near London, Ontario, that we decided to give the search for Fred another try. The photo in the *London Free Press* showed me holding Fred's photo once again, and asking if anyone recognized this veteran named Fred.

Fred's widow, Marian Gates, saw the story and called her daughter, who lived in the same village. Within an hour, our telephone rang and we were invited to come over to Alvinston, an hour's ride from Lambeth.

Mother and daughter were waiting for us, and on the kitchen table was a photo album with Fred's photo — the same one we had travelled with across Canada.

The first words Marian said were, "I am not surprised. I had my suspicions all along. After we were married in 1947, Fred kept writing to people he stayed with in Holland, so he told me."

Marian described how she knew he was writing to a woman, but he would destroy the letters so she didn't know who. She was never allowed to go to the mailbox that stood by the side of the road at the end of the driveway. "When Fred came home from work he would read the mail outside, and when he came in he would throw the letter in the wood stove," she explained.

Fred and Marian knew each other before he joined the army. He had worked part time at her father's hardware store, but Marian was too young to be dating then. When Fred returned from the war, they married. Like Johnny's mother, she was also sixteen when her first child was born. Marian, her four daughters and three sons, and their children welcomed Johnny with open arms into their family as one of their own. That Christmas, Johnny and his wife flew to Canada, and most of his father's family were at the airport to meet them. We were also invited to the reunion, and seldom have we seen such an emotional scene at the airport: there were teary eyes and grins and hugs and kisses galore!

After the airport, there was a big party at their home with all the family and friends. It was something we will never forget. Television cameras, newspaper reporters and lots of curious people! The next day, the story of Johnny's search made headlines in the newspapers across Canada: "Yes, Johnny, there is a Santa Claus."

More than fifteen years later, this family is still very close. Johnny and Rose go to Canada almost every year and, of course, the Canadian family comes to Holland for vacations. Years ago, when one of Johnny's half-brothers passed away, Marian insisted that Johnny come to Canada to be with the family and help organize things. He is now the oldest son in the family and very proud of it.

Johnny's mother was not happy that he found his Canadian family, for in doing so Johnny also discovered that his mother had lied to him all his life. Johnny has tried to explain how important it is for him to have traced his Canadian roots, but she does not understand, and the relationship between mother and son has been strained.

The search for Johnny's father, Fred, ended at the cemetery in Alvinston, Ontario. The World War II veteran died of bone-marrow cancer and was buried in 1963 at age thirty-eight.

Johnny Bruggenkamp (second left) at his first meeting with his Canadian family.

They Let Her Down
by Olga Rains

Mia lived in Holland, close to the German border, when World War II began and, like all the other young girls, she was put to work doing forced labour for the Germans.

Mia's job was in a German factory, just across the border. She would work from seven in the morning till seven in the evening and would get a ride in an army truck back to the centre of the village where she lived. Tired and hungry, Mia would arrive home and take care of a sick mother and her five younger brothers and sisters. She worked until bedtime almost every day.

Mia and Roy in happier times. When Roy went back to Canada, thoughts of Mia and their little baby drifted away.

In 1942, Mia's mother died after a two-year illness. With no one else to care for the children, Mia asked if she could stop her forced-labour job. With the help of her doctor, Mia was able to get three days a week away from the factory.

Soon after Mia was granted this exemption, her father was forced to leave his family to work in Germany. He was gone until 1944, then came home sick, another burden of care for Mia to take on.

After the Liberation, Mia met Ray, a good-looking Canadian soldier. They dated and fell in love, and a month later Mia knew that she was pregnant. Ray had signed up for Japan, so he would have to leave soon. They went to the army padre and asked permission for marriage before Ray would have to leave.

The padre advised the young couple to wait. He said it was the best thing to do, just in case Ray were killed — she would end up being a widow! Mia and Ray tried very hard to make the padre understand that they were serious, but nothing helped. They were turned down.

Ray sent parcels containing baby clothes as soon as he arrived back home in Canada. He made plans for Mia to come to Canada and filled out the necessary papers. In the meantime, Mia tried to get another member of the family to take over her job of looking after the younger brothers and sisters because her father was very ill. When word finally came that she could get passage on a boat, Mia was eight months pregnant and it was too late for her to travel. In March 1946, her little girl, Lydi, was born. She was a pretty and healthy baby.

In Canada, Ray's family had talked him into investing the money he would receive from the army. They had bought a restaurant and wanted him to be a partner. The restaurant took all his money, so instead of getting ready for Mia to join him, he had to work and build up a business.

Mia was still looking after her family, and she had to work three days a week in order to support herself and Lydi. Lydi's life got off to a bad start: so many different babysitters when she needed the love of her mother. Meanwhile, letters from Ray were few and far between. He and Mia were drifting apart.

Then Mia starting dating Peter, a Dutch fellow she knew from school. She was young, but there was no joy in life. Mia wrote to Ray and told him about Peter. Ray asked her to wait. He promised to come to Holland and marry her and take them both back to Canada "someday."

Lydi at her first confirmation. She bears a strong resemblance to her father.

This made Mia mad. Why "someday"? she asked. Lydi needed a father now. Mia stopped writing to Ray.

When Peter proposed marriage, Mia said yes, and when Lydi was five years old they got married. For a few years they were a happy family, and then the problems started. Peter began to drink more and more, and all the money he earned went for booze. When he began to hit Lydi, mother and daughter moved out and never went back.

Mia got a job in a ladies' clothing store, and she and Lydi lived in a nice apartment. The only problem was that she worked long hours and Lydi had to go to babysitters after school and on Saturdays. Lydi had too much freedom for a teenager, and when she was fifteen she became pregnant. Lydi and her boyfriend got married and the marriage seemed to work. Their little girl was born, and two years later they had a little boy. When the children went to school, Lydi and her husband both worked and they were happy together. Lydi had a very sweet and easygoing character, always willing to help anyone who needed her. She was liked by everyone and was a hard worker like her mother.

In 1980, at age thirty-four, Lydi decided to look for her Canadian father. She had a photo of him, and her mother had an old address and his service number. Lydi wrote to the Department of Veterans Affairs in Edmonton, and they told her they were not allowed to give her his address in case he was married. So instead, they gave her the address of the Legion's magazine, where Lydi placed an ad about her search for her father. One of Ray's friends read the ad and contacted him.

Mother and daughter were overjoyed to get that phone call from Canada. Ray wanted them to come over at once. Three weeks later Mia and Lydi flew to Edmonton, where Ray was waiting at the airport with flowers for both of them.

Ray had never married and had always hoped that someday he could marry Mia. Why he had never contacted Mia and Lydi, no one knows.

The three of them had a glorious three weeks together, and Ray asked Mia to marry him. He wanted to come to Holland the following summer and marry in the village where they met. Plans were made for the wedding and a date was set, but two days before Ray was to fly to Holland, he was killed in a car accident.

It took a long time for mother and daughter to get over that blow. In the meantime, Lydi's marriage was falling apart and the children were getting into trouble. Lydi's daughter married young to get away from home, and her son made the wrong friends. He began to gamble and lost money, getting himself in debt. Then he began to steal.

Her husband lost interest in their son, and Lydi's life became hellish. She tried everything she could think of to get help, but it was too late: her son committed suicide by jumping from the apartment building where they lived. Six months later, Lydi's husband left her for someone else. It was the end of the world for Lydi.

Everyone she knew wanted to help, and Lydi was determined to carry on the best she could. Fortunately, she did have her daughter, who loved and helped her. Lydi joined a church, which seemed to give her the strength she needed, and everything went fine for a while. Then she had a brain hemorrhage and was in a coma for two weeks. She came out of it, and after a year she was almost back to normal; but then she discovered alcohol. Lydi had never taken a drink in her life, so she had no idea of what alcohol can do. It made her feel relaxed, and for the first time she was able to talk about all her problems.

She seemed so happy that no one noticed how much she drank until it was too late. Lydi became sicker and sicker until there was nothing the doctors could do. Lydi's husband was at her bedside when she died. Her last words to him were, "I still love you."

A Happy Story
by Hans Kingma

My name is Hans Kingma and I was born in Holland. I grew up in the city of The Hague, and although the years after the war were not easy, it was the same for most Dutch people.

When I was sixteen, I accidentally stumbled upon some papers and found out that my parents had married three years after I was born. Nowadays, that would not be a big issue, but back then it was definitely a taboo.

I confronted my parents with the documents, and my dad confessed that I was a child born out of a relationship between my mother and a Canadian soldier. At the time, she hadn't met my stepfather yet, and she was truly convinced that this soldier was the love of her life. My mother said that she did not know he was already married in Canada, and I believe her.

Hans Kingma found his family in the Ottawa Valley.

I didn't do anything with this knowledge — I just continued with my life — but my Canadian father was always in the back of my mind. Deep down I wondered what he looked like, what kind of a man he was. There were so many questions for which I did not have any answers, but there seemed little I could do about it.

Later, when I had children of my own, they wanted to know the whole story. I guess they were curious about their roots. One day my youngest daughter heard a radio show featuring Olga Rains, and she started the ball rolling by contacting Olga. I pressured my mother into giving me as much information as she could, and she reluctantly told me his name. That was enough for Olga and Lloyd. Within one month they found my family in Canada. My natural father had passed away a long time ago, but there were eleven siblings alive in Ontario's Ottawa Valley.

In the fall of 1988, I wrote a letter to my oldest brother in Canada presenting myself as a half-brother to him and his brothers and sisters. I tell you that writing such a letter is not easy. You don't want to hurt anybody's feelings. But within a couple of weeks I received a very welcoming letter with lots of pictures of my dad and all eleven siblings. From that moment on I have been a member of the family. They found a striking resemblance between us and they have welcomed me and my family into their homes as we have for them in Holland.

I have been to Canada six times now over the last ten years and it has always felt like coming home. We share their good times and sometimes, alas, we share the bad times which inevitably come to every family. I can honestly say we have become richer in many ways and are much more aware of the importance of having family you can call your own.

The Hope and Disappointment of a Liberation Child
by Theo Timmer

I must have been fourteen years old when my niece told me that my real father was a Canadian soldier. Even then, I could see the pieces of the puzzle fall into place, but I didn't know what to do about it. I couldn't talk to my parents; I was just a teenager and I had too much respect for them. I promised my niece that I wouldn't say anything about it to anyone and I kept my word for many years.

When I got older, I met the girl of my dreams and we fell in love. We wanted to marry, and a birth certificate was required, so I applied for one. Was I in for a big surprise! On my birth certificate it said that my stepfather "acknowledged" me at age four. It stated that I was born in Breda, a city a long way from where I lived.

Theo Timmer was a cute little baby boy. It took him many years before he found out the truth about his birth and early years.

After all those years of silence, I felt that this was the time to ask my mother a few questions. She broke down in tears and told me that I was born in Moederheil, a home for unwed mothers, especially girls who were expecting Canadian babies. Breda was a long distance from Groningen, where my mother lived at the time and where she had met my father.

That is all she told me. No name, nothing else. She reminded me that I had to think about my stepfather, who had been so good to me, and she was right about that. The years went by — marriage, children, studies, my job. The mystery of my Canadian father kept gnawing at me, but with so little information, what could I do?

I tried talking to my mother again. I was now thirty-five years old. She did not want to tell me anything, and further questions would have only spoiled the relationship. My stepfather was not included in these conversations. Later, when I talked to her family, they told me that she had a traumatic time after the Liberation. When most people were celebrating, she was enduring misery.

In 1978, I realized that I had to do something to get to the bottom of my roots. I went to Breda City Hall with my passport to get information regarding my birth. There I found out the address of the home for unwed mothers where I was born, Moederheil, some dates and the name of the nun who had registered me at the City Hall.

I found out that Moederheil was no more. The name of the nun was such a common one, but I searched anyway. After a while, I gave up. Thinking I had nothing to lose, I approached my mother's brother. It was a bit risky, but I was sure that he could tell me more. He would only say that my mother had disappeared from the face of the earth in 1945 and no one in the family knew where she was. Some years later, she appeared again with a child. My uncle told me she had been 250 kilometres away, on the other side of Holland.

The years went by, and in 1999 I saw a program on TV about someone who was looking for files that had been in Moederheil, the place I was born. These files were now at another organization, so I called and they told me that I had to apply by mail, so I did. Some weeks later, I received a letter and an invitation to come and look through the archives.

Trudy Remkes, Theo's mother, in a photo taken in the 1940s. Trudy suffered terribly for the sin of having a baby out of wedlock.

94

There I was met by a friendly lady who had already made copies of my file, and to my surprise there were letters my grandfather had written to Moederheil and to the Catholic Church. It was very sad for me to read what was in them, and for the first time in my life I realized the hell my mother had gone through.

My grandfather, the nuns at Moederheil, and the church had banded together and decided that I had to be separated from my mother as soon as possible and be given up for adoption. The only good thing in the papers was the name of my biological father, the place he lived and the name of his regiment. Finally I had his name: R.L. Bellingham (not his real name) and now I could begin the search.

I started by standing alongside the big parade in Apeldoorn which is held every five years, and as all the Canadian liberators marched by I held up a big sign with my father's name on it.

All I got out of that was a few smiles, a few sneers and some turned heads. Nothing else. I had to find out more about him, but how? I wanted to know what he looked like. I wanted to meet him while he was still alive. He was getting older, and chances were he had already died. With each passing day I became more determined to find my Canadian roots.

I took the electronic highway and started in Ontario, Canada. I spent days and days behind my computer, looking for people with the name Bellingham. When I had 500 of them I sent each one an e-mail with my information. One of them had to be a family member, I thought. Day after day I received e-mails back from people from all walks of life. Some wished me luck, others gave me advice, but there was nothing about my Canadian father.

At the end of 2000, my mother's health was failing, and once again I asked her about my Canadian father. But instead of giving me more information, she accused me of bothering her. She told me that his name was not Bellingham. She claimed to have "made it up" in those days because people asked her so many questions! She only knew his first name — Wally — and that he came from British Columbia. She wouldn't tell me any more than that, saying it was a "drama" that she didn't want any part of.

There was nothing else I could do. A few weeks later, on January 6, 2001, my mother passed away. When they closed her coffin, I said to myself, "There go all my secrets."

After the funeral, we cleared out my mother's house. I had hoped to find some photos or information about my father, but there was nothing at all. I did find some old family photos and made some bundles for my cousins, whom I had not seen for years. This was to change my luck, because after a few days I received a phone call from one of them. She was older than me and remembered everything that happened at the time of my birth. The story she told me helped me to finally understand my mother.

My mother was the youngest of a family of eight children and raised in a strict Catholic family. My grandfather had an upholstering business in the centre of Groningen and was well known in this Catholic neighbourhood. I think this had much to do with what happened to my mother. When visitors came to the house, her parents locked her in the closet.

In the winter of 1946, my mother was put into a girls' home in Hoogeveen. There she had to do heavy housework, all alone in solitary confinement. In the evening and over the weekends, they locked her in a small room. This time was very traumatic for my mother, and it stayed with her for the rest of her life.

A few months before I was born, she was sent to Breda, on the other side of Holland, to a place called Moederheil, which was run by the nuns. It wasn't much better there. She had to go to church twice a day and ask God for forgiveness because she had sinned. All day long the nuns would remind the pregnant girls how sinful they were for having Canadian babies. Just before she gave birth, my mother sensed that her baby would be taken away for adoption. No one talked about it or asked her for an opinion, but she could feel that something was very wrong. My aunt, my mother's eldest sister, lived far away in The Hague and she heard what was being planned. With her last bit of money she took a train and went to Moederheil to rescue my mother and me.

As I understand it, it was not easy to get us away from the nuns as the Catholic Church, and my grandparents had forbidden the baby from being removed. It took years before the relationship between my aunt and the rest of the family was normal again. Secrets were kept airtight in those days. There are still people in my family who know nothing about this.

After hearing this story from my cousin, I finally understood what my mother meant when she said the story of my birth was a "drama." My aunt had saved me from being adopted.

I felt so bad. I had never known this. As far as I was concerned, she was just another aunt, and I had so many of them. It was a very emotional experience, talking to my cousin and discovering the circumstances of my birth.

But there was still one thing I needed to know, and only my aunt would know the answer. What was the real name of my father? "Bellingham," she replied.

Now I knew for sure. What to do next? One of my family in Groningen had seen an article about Lloyd and Olga Rains and the work they did for the Liberation children in Holland. They also had a website. I contacted Project Roots, and a week or so later my story and photos were on their site. That was in April 2001. Five months later, I received an e-mail that Project Roots had found an R.L. Bellingham in England.

My birth certificate said L.R. Bellingham. The first two initials were the same, but turned around — on purpose or by mistake? Who knows? All that mattered was the Rains had found my father! I was overjoyed. It was the happiest day of my life. I could not believe that he was still alive.

The Rains told me not to do anything until they had contacted him. A week later, they wrote me that the contact was made and that he did not want anything to do with me. He claimed to be scared to death of what his wife and peers would think of him.

The Rains just happened to be in Canada at that time, and they kept trying to set up an appointment for me to meet my father, to make him understand, but all they got was an earful of excuses. He reluctantly agreed to meet me, but only under protest, in front of the Canadian Embassy in London on October 24, 2001.

I decided to go to England a few days earlier than the day I was supposed to meet my father. I had his address, so I wanted to see where he lived and what kind of a life he led. I was very impressed with his home in Normandy. He has done well for himself in England.

On October 24, 2001, I went with my twenty-eight-year-old daughter, who speaks very good English, to the Canadian Embassy in London. We did not want to be late, so we there half an hour early. He was half an hour late due to a traffic jam, but I had no way of knowing this, so an hour after I had arrived I was getting very nervous. All sorts of thoughts raced through my mind — "Maybe he is not coming after all."

I saw several veterans going to the desk to report that they had arrived. I went over and asked them if Mr. Bellingham was coming and they said yes. Then I saw him. He walked in with another veteran and he looked around, so I went over to him and asked if he was Mr. Bellingham. He wanted me to come outside, and there we stood, on the steps of the Canadian Embassy, father and son, for the very first time.

He looked very unfriendly to me. He looked like he wanted to say, "Well, what do you want?"

I asked him some questions and he kept looking at his watch, which made me more nervous. Then he mentioned that he had to be inside very soon. He could not remember much about the things I asked him. When I showed him my mother's wartime photo, he looked away. I know that he lied about most things I asked him. First, he said he was never in Groningen, then later he said that he had been there for a dance. He kept telling me that he was not my father, but I felt more and more that he was. I was so disappointed and got angry, told him that we should have a DNA test to be sure, even if the cost was high. I was thinking of pulling a few hairs from his head.

All of a sudden he looked at me — he looked very frightened — and said, "Okay. I am your father." I shook his hand, but at the same time I felt as if I was going to disappear into the ground. There we stood, his Dutch son and his crying granddaughter. Thank God the weather was nice — it was the only good thing about that day.

He told me that he had no children and that he had been married for fifty-four years and that further contact was impossible. He said that if his wife found out about me, she would either divorce him or would die due to her frail health. I had to solemnly swear that I would never contact him again.

He told me that he was a poor Canadian veteran and had been a house painter in his younger years. He saw me as a rich Dutchman having a good life — how else could I afford a trip to England? After that he said something that made me feel like dirt. In his opinion, there were no virgins amongst the Dutch women in those days.

Very disappointed, I brought the conversation to an end after fifteen minutes because he kept looking at his watch. He had to attend a meeting for Canadian veterans. It is now a few weeks after the meeting with my biological father and I still do not know anything about him. And again the gnawing starts. What kind of man is my father? Why isn't he more understanding towards me? I can't help that I was born, and I have not blamed him for anything. What I do understand is that he is not as poor as he wants me to believe. I think he would have a lot of explaining to do to his wife. He told me that he was married right after the war ended, which means that he was already married when he met my mother.

He is living in a small village, and I think people look up to him because he is involved with a group of Canadians and also has another function in that village. He could lose his "good" reputation if they found out about me. He must have trusted me when I promised him that I would never get in touch with his wife. He did not object to some photos being taken. All I have now are four photos of a stranger — not a father — but my search is not over. I am determined to find out if he has children. Hopefully they will have more compassion than their father.

I never thought it could end up this way. I have heard of so many other fathers who embrace their war children, and of other children who don't even know their father's name and will never have any knowledge of the Canadian father or his family. Still, I am happy that I have come this far and that I have met the man who fathered me. Without Project Roots and Olga and Lloyd Rains, this would have never happened.

Postscript: Since meeting his father in London, Theo has found out he has a half-sister and two half-brothers — twins — who are also in their fifties. He received two friendly letters from one of his brothers in 2002. Theo had hoped that they could meet in person, but so far a reunion has not taken place.

Nel's Perseverence Paid Off!
by Olga Rains

Nel was born in Amsterdam in 1946, a child of the Liberation. Her Canadian father, Ron, and her Dutch mother, Jenny, fell in love and dated for about four months. Ron was repatriated to Canada and, like so many other soldiers, he left his pregnant girlfriend behind.

Nel lived with her grandparents in Amsterdam and although she knew who her real mother was, Jenny was treated like an older sister. One day at a birthday party when she was about twelve years old, she overheard a conversation about a Canadian friend Jenny had after the war. Nel put two and two together, and when she asked Jenny about the Canadian soldier, she was told he had been killed during the war.

Nothing more was said about it until years later, when Nel overheard Jenny and an aunt talking about the Canadian again. Nel had a feeling that her father might still be alive, so she asked once more. This time she was shown a photo of her parents in the centre of Amsterdam in 1945.

After Jenny passed away in 1976, Nel's aunt told her the whole story about Ron and Jenny. Apparently, Ron knew that Jenny was pregnant. His parents wrote a letter to Jenny, telling her that Ron wanted to take responsibility for the baby and that he still wanted to marry her, despite the fact that there already was a marriage arranged in Canada with another woman.

Nel's parents in a photo taken in Amsterdam following the Liberation.

The letter went on to say that if Jenny came to Canada, the other marriage would not happen. It was a strange letter, and Jenny wondered why Ron hadn't written it. After all, he was a soldier who had fought a war; he didn't need his parents to write letters for him. It was all so confusing. Under pressure from her mother, Jenny decided not to go to Canada.

That was the end of her relationship with Ron.

As the years passed and Nel grew up into an adult with children of her own, she tried everything to find her father. She followed up on every lead and, being an outgoing, friendly person, she soon had people in both Holland and Canada helping her. Still, nothing happened.

In 1995, during the celebration of the fiftieth anniversary of the Liberation, many Canadian veterans came to Holland. Nel stood alongside the parade in Apeldoorn with a big sign that read, "My dad is Roy Stanly. Who knows him?"

Nothing came of this so Nel decided to continue her search in Canada. She found her way to radio and television stations and told her story to different newspapers but after three weeks of travelling through Ontario she returned, disappointed, to Holland. Was she ever going to find her father?

Then one day she stopped by the library and looked through books about World War II. There were many of them, so she spent some days looking for a photo of her father so that she could find out what regiment he had been with.

She did find a photo of a tank with several soldiers, and one of them looked very much like her father! The photo was taken during the Liberation of Ermelo in Holland. Nel wrote to the newspaper in Ermelo, asking if anyone could remember which regiment the tank was connected with. She got an answer, and someone gave her the address of the former commander of that regiment.

He did not know a Roy Stanly, but did have an R.E. Staly on his list, and even though it was a different spelling, it might be him. The commander knew someone who had a museum with all kinds of information about the war, and he offered to find out something about this veteran. As it turned out, Nel had the wrong spelling of her father's name. In 1997, Mr. R.E. Staly was found. The first phone call was very emotional; three weeks later, Nel went to Canada with her daughter to meet the man she had been looking for all her life.

When Nel called to let him know she was coming, he was very scared. This was all going much too fast for him; he was not a well man, he said. Nel wondered if he felt guilty. After all, he had never looked for her. It was she who had spent most of her life trying to find him. But this was not the time to turn back. Putting her doubts aside, Nel made up her mind to see her father in Canada.

After the first big hug, Nel and her dad both knew they were going to be very happy! Ron was a lonely man, and meeting Nel brightened up his life. He lived all by himself, having divorced his wife forty years earlier, and his only son died at the age of forty-four. On the day that Nel arrived, his son would have been fifty.

Every year, Nel and her husband went to Canada to visit her Canadian dad. A few years ago, he died, and Nel went over for the funeral. Nel brought his ashes back to Holland, and his urn sits on the mantle in her living room.

Nel looked for her father for more than 35 years and when she finally found him in Canada it was a happy reunion for all.

It Happened for a Reason
by Leona (Lorna) Tange

My name is Leona Tange. After Belgium was liberated by the Allies in 1944, I found a job working for the British Army. The sergeant-major could not pronounce my name so he called me Lorna instead. Ever since then, I have been known as Lorna.

My story begins in 1942, when I graduated from school and married a Belgian man. Within a year, my first child, a daughter named Ilse, was born. Two years later, I couldn't stand my husband's abuse any longer, so I fled to my parents' home and took the baby with me. I was twenty-one years old.

By then, Liberation was already a fact in Belgium, and British troops were stationed in Ghent. I knew four languages and bookkeeping, so I got a job working for the British military.

In 1945 I met Gerry, a Canadian soldier stationed in Ghent. At first we were just friends, but before I knew it, we were in love. I remember his smile and the respect he gave me after what I had been through with my husband. I can still see him standing at the gate of my office when I finished work. On our walk home he would hum a tune.

By April 1945, I was pregnant with Gerry's child. Since I wasn't legally divorced, marrying Gerry was out of the question. I was very worried about my parents. What would they say?

In July, Gerry's company moved from Ghent to Gavere. We said goodbye but the same night he came back, drunk. He told me he had deserted and had plans for us to go together to France. I always had a great respect for the law and justice. I wouldn't even think of living with a deserter in a foreign country, so I persuaded Gerry to give himself up. To be certain that he did, I brought him to the barracks myself. He was sentenced to detention in England until his return to Canada.

I went to the coast and started as supervisor in the Naafi — the casino in Blankenberghe. At the end of August they closed, and I went to Tournai. I worked as a clerk/telephone operator with the British Transport Company until all the troops left Belgium in 1946. Every weekend, I took the train to Ghent to see Ilse, my little girl, and to pay my mom for her upkeep. Usually, I laced my corset tight and wore a loose-fitting coat I had made from a sleeping bag.

It was eight months before my mother noticed that I was pregnant. She never forgave me for it. She was furious and told me what a disgrace I was and how ashamed she was to be my mother. My mother was a good woman but a child born out of wedlock — and by a Canadian soldier — was something she could not take.

On Christmas Eve 1945, the contractions started. The British did not pay sick leave, so I went to work anyway, thinking I could make it through the day. But when my co-workers saw that I was in pain, they urged me to go to the hospital and asked if there was a family member who could attend. I was embarrassed to tell them the truth, so I left work right away and went to my tiny room, where I waited for the baby's time to come. In the middle of the night, I gathered my things together for the hospital and walked silently with my little suitcase full of clothes for me and the baby.

The clinic was only fifteen minutes from my place, but it took me two hours to get there. I had to cross the park, and I saw shadows behind every tree. I was so afraid and lonely, but I did not cry. Arriving at the door of the hospital, I looked through the keyhole but did not dare to ring the bell. I stood there for a long time until I could no longer bear the pain and, finally, I rang for help. In the morning, Ann Patricia was born, weighing 3.3 kilograms. She was a healthy little girl.

The day I left the hospital, a relative of my father's came and invited me to rest for a few days at her place. I was very grateful, not realizing that this was the start of the struggle for my daughter. The relatives who had so kindly offered me assistance had plans for my baby. They wanted to keep her. I had to ask permission for everything concerning Patricia — to take her for a walk or to give her a bath. I should have stood up to them, but I had no authority when it came to my own child.

The winter of 1946 was very cold, with lots of snow. I had a stove but no coal. Everything was still rationed using coupons, and I had to give mine to my mother for Ilse. I made myself a house coat from an army blanket to keep warm at night. I can still feel the cold of that winter.

Meantime, Gerry was released from military service and sent back to Canada. He wrote regularly, and so did his mother and Yvonne — a French-Canadian girl who was engaged to his brother. No one ever told me that when Gerry returned to Canada, he had to marry a girl who had become pregnant with his baby. I also found out after my father died in 1968 that Gerry had written a letter to him after Patricia was born. In the letter he wrote what a wonderful girl I was and what a good mother I was going to be when we got married.

Jan. 13, 1946
On Active Service
Pte. Gerry ———
4 C.M.P. & D.B.
Canadian Army Overseas

Dear Sir,

Lorna has asked me to write to you so I will do so immediately. She has probably told you quite a bit about me as it is. We have never been introduced but I do know you to see you. I have met your wife several times at the house so I'm acquainted with half of the family anyways

A letter is rather an impersonal way to introduce myself but that is the only way under present conditions. However, I expect to come to Belgium within the next month so maybe then I'll have the pleasure of meeting you.

I received the news the other day that Lorna gave birth to an eight-pound baby girl and was very pleased to hear. As you probably know, I sent her a certificate and claimed paternity to the child. I'm going to marry Lorna at the earliest convenience. I know there are certain complications before I do so, but I am sure we can manage them. Lorna is a wonderful girl and will make a wonderful wife and mother. I do hope this meets your approval. I also hope you will not hold any ill findings against either one of us.

We planned everything before I left Belgium so now it's just a matter of time. At the present time I am in England and have been here for the past seven months but I should be leaving soon. After I come to Belgium I will be returning to Canada to be discharged from the Army. Then I will be coming to Belgium to claim Lorna and take her home with me. I wrote to my own family and explained everything and they seem very pleased at my intentions.

Have any of you been down to see her lately? From my news she is doing quite well, that is a consolation any way. This will be all for now. Hoping to hear from you soon.

Respectfully yours,

Gerry ———

P.S. I hope you all spent a very pleasant Xmas and New Years. We done pretty well over here. Give my regard to the family.

By 1948, I was back living with my parents. When Patricia was two and a half years old, I asked the relatives if I could take her for a holiday to the coast with me. Instead, I took Pat to my parents' home in Ghent, where I planned to take care of her myself. My mother let me know right away that she had no intention of looking after both Pat and Ilse while I was at work.

That Monday, I had to go to work. I brought Pat and Ilse to the infant school and on Tuesday to the same program in the morning. At about eleven in the morning my youngest brother came to my office to warn me that Pat had been taken by the relatives. If I wanted my daughter back, I had to pay them for the two years she was in their care. That week I tried in vain to get a loan — impossible for a single woman. Pat grew up with the relatives and I had no say in the matter.

My letters to Gerry went to his mother's address. We corresponded for several years. Gerry made no promises — of course he could not, since he was married to another woman in Canada, but I didn't know it at the time. I remember sending him a photo when I was twenty-five, and he wrote that I was still looking very well despite everything I had been through. Then, suddenly, in 1949, he stopped writing.

Two years passed, then one day in 1951 I received a letter from his sister, Trudy. She confessed that the reason Gerry stopped writing was that she had intercepted my letters. Gerry thought I wasn't interested in him, so he stopped writing. Trudy also told me that Gerry had got another girl pregnant and he was talking of joining up to fight in Korea.

I implored Trudy to tell Gerry not to let a second girl down. The message must have got back to him, because shortly thereafter I got a call from him, asking if I there was still a chance for us. I was so hurt from Trudy's letter and everything that had happened that I lashed out at him. "Do you have to waste all that money on a long-distance telephone call to ask me that?" He hung up the phone and I never heard from him again.

In April 1953, my youngest brother married and some of his friends came to the wedding. One of the guests was Sam, a tall, handsome fellow in American uniform. Sam and I married on July 10, 1954, and we have had a good life together, but my relationship with Pat has always been rocky. It would take a whole book to write about all the humiliations, the million painful barbs I had to endure during Pat's childhood from family and later from her own maliciousness. All the blame for everything that happened after the war was focused on me.

When Pat became an adult, she asked me to help find her real father. I never really gave it much thought, but then one day I heard about Olga and Lloyd Rains of Project Roots. With their help I got Gerry's address as well as his sister Trudy's. Patricia wrote a letter to her father, but he did not respond, so I wrote to Trudy asking her to intervene. Trudy answered my letter, and since then her other sister Marie and I also struck up a relationship by mail. Through them, I have learned about Gerry's life after the war and I am glad we did not marry. He was an alcoholic in Canada and we probably would not have lasted. "You did not miss out on anything," his sister said to me.

Looking back now, I think Gerry was a coward. He lied to me about our plans to marry and then he hid his marriage in Canada. But there is plenty of blame to go around. My parents did not really support me during the difficult times and my relatives took away Pat, causing so much bitterness. Trudy held back my letters in 1949 and that did not bode well for a relationship with Gerry. But maybe it all happened for a reason.

It took many years, but eventually Pat and I reconciled and now she remembers my birthday and sends New Year's and Christmas cards. She has come to visit and even calls me Mama. I wonder if, after nearly sixty years, she has finally accepted the things we cannot change?

As for me, I don't ask too many questions. I am just glad to finally have my daughter back and to enjoy the last years of my life knowing what happened after the war with Gerry, Pat and my family was not all in vain.

Lorna and Olga Rains. Lorna's life was never the same after she had a child by a Canadian soldier.

I Had a Happy Reunion with My Father in Canada
by Simonne Gallis

The first time I talked to my father, my heart nearly burst with joy. Those two words, "Hello, Simonne," meant so much to me, for they marked the end of a lifelong search for my dad.

We talked about his health and his family, and halfway through the conversation I asked him if I could call him "Dad." He said yes and told me this was the best present he ever received in his life. There was much happiness and emotion, and "I love you" was said many times back and forth.

So ended the first conversation with my Canadian dad.

In the days that followed I was very happy, but then I started to have doubts about his honesty. I had surprised him with my phone call, and what else could he do but be friendly to the daughter he had left behind in Belgium after World War II?

Nothing my husband Danny said would allay my fears. I did not sleep for two nights, and stayed close to the telephone, but I didn't have the nerve to dial his number. The thought that I would make a fool of myself and spoil everything stopped me from making that call.

All kinds of thoughts went through my head, and it nearly drove me crazy. If he loved me so much, why did he never try to find me? I decided to call and get it over with. But just before I picked up the phone it rang, and on the other end of the line was my father. "This is your dad. I couldn't wait any longer to hear your voice again, Simonne," he said.

Simonne's father in a wartime photo. He wanted to marry Simonne's mother, but she refused.

Tears were streaming down my face. We talked and talked. He told me he had one son, an only child. I was also an only child, so I knew what he was going through, always being alone.

I wanted to see my dad and brother as soon as I could. My father was in good health, but we already had missed so many good years of our lives together and there were many unanswered questions. My mother had always told me bad things about my father. Now I would see for myself if they were true.

I was fourteen years old when I found out that my father was a Canadian soldier. It was the Christmas holidays and I was home alone. My mother and stepfather were both out working. While looking for some old school books in the attic, I found a box that had a string tightly wrapped around it.

Of course, my curiosity got the better of me and I took the box close to the small window where I could see it better. I loosened the knot in the string, took it off and lifted the lid. I had the shock of my life! There was a photo of my father, a Canadian soldier. There were letters to my mother, but my English was not very good then so I just skimmed over them. Several times I read the words "baby girl" and I knew he was writing about me.

I never mentioned anything to my mother for another three years. Then, when I was seventeen, I had a boyfriend, and my parents did not approve of him. This made me mad, and one evening when I returned home from a date, my stepfather started to give me a speech about my boyfriend.

I told him that it was none of his business what I did, that I had known the secret about my real father for three years. He couldn't tell me what to do.

This time it was my mother's world that turned upside down. I thought she would tell me what had happened and why she did not marry my father, but she never did. She always painted my father black, accusing him of flirting and going out with another girl while he was dating her.

What I found out was the opposite: my dad fought around Nymegen in Holland and after the war was over he came back to Belgium to marry my mother. The announcement was posted in the Catholic Church. Then someone told Dad that she had been going out with English soldiers who were stationed in her city while he was fighting in Holland. My father still wanted to marry my mother, if only to give me his name, but she refused!

Who was wrong and who was right? I will never know, and who cares now? I am fifty-five years old. Do we blame everything on World War II and the moral standards that were formed during the Nazi occupation?

In the meantime, while I was planning my trip to Canada, something happened that I never expected. My mother found out that I had contacted my father and she managed to get his address from my address book. I trusted my mother; otherwise, I would not have left my book lying around where she could find it. She wanted revenge on me because I was planning to fly to Canada and see my father; she found another person in Canada who became her spy.

She called this person and together they made a plan to call my father's family and say things about him that were not true. They also planned to get information out of his Canadian family so they could run back to me with it. I often wonder what kind of person that man was, to do such a dirty job for someone he didn't even know.

As you can imagine, this caused a serious commotion in my dad's family and made it hard for me to go through with my trip to Canada. My mother had ruined my plans.

Fortunately, her Canadian spy did not come across as very trustworthy or professional, so when my dad talked to his family, he figured out who was behind it all. My father called and told me not to worry, the family knew all about my mother's machinations.

My first trip to Canada was in January 1992. While flying over this huge country, many thoughts went through my mind. I felt so alone, and a bit scared of what was to come. But as the flight came to an end, I had the sense that I was going home.

After we landed, all I could see was lots of snow. Everything looked like a Christmas card. At the airport, I could see my dad from a distance, waiting among a crowd of people, trying to get a glimpse of me. When he finally gathered me in his arms, I knew this man was my dad. It was like a magnetic power that drew us together. All the worry and fear were gone.

I was very impressed with the beauty of Canada — the serenity, the endless prairies with snow. I noticed that there were no birds, no bicycles, no motor bikes; now and then a car or a truck and, of course, snow plows to keep the roads clean. We had to keep scraping the windows on the inside because our breath froze them up. It was thirty below zero outside!

In the weeks to come, my brother Gerry, Dad and I did a lot of talking. We found out that we had a lot in common. After my mother refused to marry him, my father married another Belgian girl, so Gerry and I both had Belgian mothers. Gerry's mother had passed away, and it was for the better — according to some of the family, she would not have accepted me.

I met many of Dad's friends and neighbours in Saskatchewan where he lives, and he also took me to his church and introduced me to his pastor and the congregation. As to be expected, we had many strange looks and lots of questions as I walked arm in arm with my dad through the village.

We told each other all about our lives. He explained what happened during the war and after when he came back to Canada. He told me why he had married Margie and not my mother. He gave me his diary to read while I was there. In his diary I read that he had been back for a visit to Belgium with Margie to visit her family and he had wanted to find out about me, but didn't have a chance.

I believe him now when he tells me that he longed for me all his life. And even though I was forty-six years old, in the arms of my dad I felt like a four-year-old, safe and secure from the world around me. One thing I know for sure, only God can separate us. I hope and pray every day that my father and I have many years together.

Sadly, now that I have found my dad, I have lost my mother. She wants nothing more to do with me.

Lloyd and Olga, thank you both for all you did for me.

Simonne (front centre) was fourteen years old when she found out that her father was a Canadian soldier. Her father is front left, brother Gerry in back and Gerry's wife to the right.

Children of War Brides
by Melynda Jarratt

"My mother would never talk about my father."

Forty-eight thousand war brides married Canadian soldiers during World War II, but not all of them came to Canada, and of those who did, not all had a fairy-tale ending to their romance. This group of war brides arrived in November 1946, on board the Lady Rodney.

In March 1947, the Directorate of Repatriation for the Canadian Department of National Defence optimistically reported that by the time all of the 48,000 war brides and their children were brought to Canada, the total number of servicemen's dependents could very well exceed 70,000.[1]

What those figures don't tell us, however, is that not all of the 48,000 marriages between Canadian servicemen and their war brides ended up in idyllic circumstances back in Canada. By February 1947, the official war bride transportation scheme was coming to a close and nearly 10 percent, or 4,500 war brides, had decided not to come to Canada despite offers of free passage by the Canadian Wives Bureau in London and the Continent.[2]

The reasons cited were varied: for instance, many Canadian husbands wanted to stay overseas, where they had spent the last five or six years. But according to the Wives Bureau, most of the wives who did not want to come to Canada did so because their "marriages have not been successful."[3]

In addition to these were about five hundred problem cases, women who, for a variety reasons including illness and pregnancy, were not expected to come to Canada at all.[4] Some of these problem cases had the decision made for them by the Immigration Branch, which refused to approve their settlement arrangements in Canada. If the destination of a war bride and child was a Salvation Army Hotel or a tar-paper shack in northern Ontario, branch officials refused their stamp of approval: "SA," for "Satisfactory Arrangements." According to Wives Bureau officials, when informed of the arrangements made for them in Canada, the vast majority of these five hundred "made their own decision not to come."[5]

Other wives and children actually did immigrate to Canada on the war bride ships, but their marriages did not survive real life in Canada. They cut their losses and, with no thanks to the Canadian government, they made their way back home with the children as soon as possible. They form part of a group for whom incompatibility, poverty and alcoholism were the common experience, and one might say these women did the right thing for their children because their lives were infinitely better back home.

Lloyd and Olga Rains on their wedding day, December 24, 1945. Eight days later, Lloyd was repatriated back to Canada and it was another eleven months before they saw each other again.

We'll never know how many women went back home to Britain and Europe after coming to Canada as war brides. Once the war emergency was over, Immigration no longer counted these women as a distinct group, so they blended into statistics for outward migration. We can only imagine how many war brides who found themselves in dire circumstances in Canada would have liked to go back, but who received no help from the Canadian government and did not have the financial resources to do so on their own.

Correspondence from a "desperate" war bride, Mrs. M.F.,[6] to the Canadian Wives Bureau in March 1947 (see page 134), as well as a letter from External Affairs about "embarrassing" situations that had occurred at its New York office, show the difficulties these women endured and the kind of help they could expect from Canadian authorities.

In an April 1947, letter to Deputy Minister of Mines and Resources Hugh Keenleyside (whose Immigration Branch was responsible for bringing the war brides to Canada), the Department of External Affairs complained that the Canadian government had to come up with a plan for women who were leaving their Canadian husbands and ending up destitute in New York as they tried to make their way back home to England.

> In the first case of these a girl was taken down to New York by her husband who was, she thought, going to accompany her back to England. In New York, however, he disappeared and the girl was left absolutely penniless in that city. In view of the publicity which is being given to ill-treated war brides in the United States, and the great lengths to which the United States authorities have gone in looking after each individual case, it would have been hard indeed for Mr. Scully to wash his hands of the case, the story of which had got into the newspapers and so on. In the end, the British Consul General stepped and on his own responsibility sent the girl home as a distressed British Merchant Seaman. We understand the Foreign Office and the Ministry of Transport have taken strong exception to this action, and that the Consul General who authorized it is being held personally responsible from his own funds.
>
> The other case was that of a girl and her baby, who missed the ship in New York and had to be held over and did not have any money to live on. Some one had to take care of them. I gather that the Saint George's Society was the benefactor in this case.[7]

Many husbands, too, abandoned their marriages in Britain and Europe after being repatriated to Canada. Given the sociocultural context of the 1940s with its "boys will be boys" attitude towards servicemen, it is not surprising that married men just walked away from their children overseas. It's the kind of attitude that would not be tolerated in young soldiers today, but it was certainly tolerated — if not accepted and encouraged — in the 1940s. The military could force a married man to pay child support to his ex-wife while he was still in its employ, but once he was repatriated, he became a veteran and the responsibility of the Department of Veterans Affairs, which did nothing to help. The mother was on her own, and nobody could force the father to pay anything from Canada without great effort and cost.

Then there are the fathers who so desperately wanted to be part of their children's lives, but whose ex-wives would have no part in it. These stories are particularly sad, because fathers tried to maintain relationships, some of them even moving back to England. Even today, with all the advantages of our modern society, the distance of geography, time and place wears down even the most committed dad when he's confronted with an intransigent custodial parent. Recent studies of divorced fathers and parental alienation syndrome point to similar findings. Given enough obstacles, eventually, a father will give up.

From the child's perspective, a recurring theme is one of loss. The psychological effect of their fathers' absence and the frustration of not knowing what really happened between their parents haunt them to this day. It is a testimony to the strength of the father-child bond that these war children, who are now in their late fifties and sixties, are driven to find their Canadian fathers and discover their roots. Here are their stories.

NOTES

1. PAC, History, Directorate of Repatriation, p. 35.

2. February 10, 1947, Memorandum, Breakdown of figures provided to the Department of Mines and Resources, Immigration Branch, by Col. Ellis, Director Repatriation, Department of National Defence, which represents the complete picture of servicemen's dependents remaining the United Kingdom and N.W.E. who may apply for free passage to Canada after the last sailing under Army auspices which arrived in Halifax, January 19, 1947. PAC, Immigration Branch RG 76 Vol 462, File 705870 pt. 10. Eight months later, the numbers hadn't changed that much, and by the time the free scheme was over in February 1948, some 64,000 souls, consisting of approximately 43,500 brides and their 21,000 children, had made their way to Canada, 6,000 fewer than had been estimated less than a year earlier.

3. December 9, 1946, Report on Problems Relating to Dependents Overseas, PAC, Immigration Branch, RG76, Vol 462, File 705870, pt. 9.

4. February 10, 1947, Memorandum.

5. December 31, 1947, "A Brief History of Servicemen's Dependents in Second World War," PAC, Immigration Branch, RG 76 Vol 462, File 705870, pt. 11.

6. PAC, Letter from M.F., Barrisfield, Kingston, Ontario, to Col. Ellis, Director of Repatriation, March 1947.

7. Letter from Laurent Beaudry, Acting Under-Secretary of State for External Affairs, to Hon. Hugh Keenleyside, Deputy Minister of Mines and Resources, April 23, 1947. PAC, Immigration Branch, RG 76 Vol 462 File 705870 pt. 10.

Desperate to Get Me Back
by Richard Bond

My father, John (Jack) Cecil Bond, was an engineer in civilian life but during the Second World War he was a sergeant in the Royal Canadian Army Service Corps stationed in Basingstoke, England. There he met and married my mother, Noreen Mary Mitchell, in March 1943.

When I was less than a year old, my mother and I went to live with my father's relatives in Quebec while he was still fighting in Italy. After some time in Quebec, my mother made the decision to return to England for good. We travelled by train to New York and crossed the Atlantic on the *Queen Elizabeth*. My mother had bought a return ticket, but she had no intention of returning to Canada. When my father realized what was going on, he caught the next boat to England, but I did not find this out until a few years ago. My mother would never talk about my father, and I knew virtually nothing about him, but I was always led to believe he went back to Canada.

This was not the case at all: my mother's sister, Aunt Joan, told me that a legal separation followed and my father was allowed access on Sundays. When my mother no longer allowed visits, he became desperate and broke into her house to get me. A court case followed, and my father was sentenced to six months incarceration. Because of good behaviour, he only served three months and spent this time working on a farm near Winchester, Hampshire.

John (Jack) Bond tried everything to have a relationship with his son, including moving back to England after his wife, a war bride, left him in Canada.

In the late 1950s, my mother rang Aunt Joan in a panic to say that my father had been to the house and was looking for me. Her cleaning lady said that, while she was out, a man had come to the door "who looked just like Richard." He said he would call again, but as far as I know, he didn't.

My mother would never speak about my father or give me any information, but I was led to believe he was not interested in me. Consequently, in the late 1960s when I was approached at work by a stranger and asked if I would be interested in contacting my father, I said, "He isn't interested in me so I am not interested in him."

It was not until years later that I found out that this was not true and came to very much regret the missed opportunity to meet him. Then a chance conversation with my mother's sister in the early 1990s changed my mind. My aunt told me that my father had been desperate to get me back and had even stayed in England for a while after my parents split up. She stayed in touch with him for a few years but did not realize that I knew absolutely nothing about him, not even what he looked like. She found an old photograph, and my wife and I decided that we would try to trace him.

It was very difficult to know where to start, and made harder by the fact that we had to keep it from my mother, who would have been furious had she found out we were looking for my father. We tried a number of places such as the Salvation Army and the Canadian Army Records office, but with no luck.

After my mother died in 1998, I decided to renew my efforts. My wife and I saw an article in a newspaper about an organization called TRACE (Transatlantic Children's Enterprise), which helps the war children of American GIs who served in England during World War II. The organization is run by Pamela Winfield of England. I wrote and asked if it extended to children of the Canadian forces. I received a brief note back recommending that I contact Olga Rains in Holland.

The Rains suggested that I place an advertisement in the Royal Canadian Legion's magazine, which I did in May 1999. As it so happens, the month previous, Project Roots launched its website and featured the search for my father as one of the main stories. In May, we went on holiday to Mexico, and on our return I had a message that someone had phoned me from Canada. I rang him straightaway and found out that he was a brother of my father. He had read the front-page article about the Project Roots website in Canada's *National Post* newspaper. On the site, he found my father's name and picture and the story of my long search for him.

The first shock was that my father had died in 1986 — in England! I found out that my father had never gone back to Canada after coming over to get me. He remarried some years later and lived in Hertfordshire, only about sixty miles from where I live. My father was one of seven children, so in addition to my uncle, I found I also have two aunts, one living in Canada and one in the United States.

In September 1999, we went to visit my uncle in Ottawa. There was a big family wedding while we were there, and a reunion was arranged for the same weekend. I found I have about forty relatives in all, and only two cousins were unable to attend the reunion. It was quite overwhelming to find I had so many relatives, and they all made me feel so welcome! We had a wonderful stay and were invited back again. In April 2000, my aunt and a cousin paid us a visit in England, and my uncle came for ten days in June. We have just returned from another visit to Canada, where we stayed with an aunt and cousins in different parts of Ontario.

Thank you, Project Roots.

Richard Bond (far right) at a September 1999 family reunion in Ontario. Richard was one of the first war children whose Canadian family was found through the Project Roots website.

Who Was Clifford Harold Sims?
by Melynda Jarratt

Jan Walker (née Philomena Sims) doesn't remember the last time she saw her father, the late Clifford Harold Sims. She doesn't know much about him, either — other than the fact that he died on March 19, 2001, at the Brock Fahrni Pavilion, a veterans' hospital located at 749 West 33rd Avenue in Vancouver, British Columbia.

But Jan believes someone must have known and cared for her father before his death in 2001. She is hoping that someone can explain why Clifford Harold Sims brought his two motherless children all the way from Britain in December 1946, only to abandon them in Regina, Saskatchewan, as soon as they arrived. The decision to give his two little girls up for adoption in

After the story of Jan's search for her sister Eileen appeared in the Regina Leader Post in December 2002, this photo and several others were mailed to her anonymously. In this snapshot, Jan and Eileen appear to be showing off their new dolls, perhaps Christmas gifts.

the confusion of the postwar years has been a mystery that has haunted Jan Walker for more than fifty-five years. And after years of fruitless searching, Jan has decided to go public with her story in the hope that someone will recognize her father's name.

Jan's story is not your typical adopted child situation: her mother, Bridget Mary (née Murphy), was one of nearly 48,000 British and European women who married Canadian soldiers overseas during World War II. The Irish-born Bridget and her daughters should have come to Canada on the war bride ships at the end of the war, but things didn't turn out the way they were supposed to. Bridget married Clifford Harold Sims in Croydon, England, on September 23, 1941. The couple had two children: Philomena (called Jan), born June 5, 1941, and Eileen, born July 31, 1942. According to a friend in England who was contacted by the Saskatchewan Social Services after the girls' arrival in Canada, Bridget was a "wonderful mother who lived for her two little girls" and they were "a very happy little trio."

Sometime in 1944, Mr. Sims was injured in a truck accident and, as was the practice for injured soldiers, he was repatriated to Canada, where he would not be a burden on Britain's strained resources. Presumably, his wife and two daughters would follow him to Canada when shipping space became available, as did some 2,000 war brides who braved the dangerous ocean voyage between 1943 and 1944.

We do not know why Bridget didn't come immediately to Canada when her husband was repatriated, but it could have been any one of a number of reasons. Due to the priority passage system, it wasn't easy for a female civilian and her children to get berthing space on a ship headed to Canada. There was always someone else, including politicians and injured Canadian soldiers, who had more important reasons to travel. It is entirely possible that Bridget was offered passage, but turned it down for fear of the German U-Boats that were roaming the Atlantic torpedoing Allied convoys.

Then there was the fact that women over six months pregnant were not allowed to travel by transatlantic ship. But Bridget would have had plenty of time to make arrangements once she found out she was pregnant in December 1943.

The Immigration Branch also had a say in whether a pregnant war bride and two young children could come to Canada to live. If the settlement arrangements were unsatisfactory — a decision that was based on a wide variety of factors, ranging from substandard housing and poverty to illness or an alcoholic husband — the family would not be allowed to travel until the situation improved.

Whatever happened, we do know that Bridget was still in England nine months later when, on August 31, 1944, she gave birth to a boy, John Philip, in Woking Maternity Hospital, Surrey. The next day, September 1, she was dead, apparently from complications due to childbirth.

With the father in Canada and no family to assist, the infant boy was placed for adoption and the two girls, Philomena and Eileen, were placed with a foster family near Portslade, Sussex. In January 1945, the girls were moved to a convent, where they stayed until December 1946. From there, they were destined to join their father in Carrot River, Saskatchewan, on the *Empire Brent* along with a ship full of war brides and children. The girls were escorted on the trip by a Red Cross

Escort Officer and, after arriving in Halifax on December 13, were brought to Regina by train. For reasons that are still unclear, the two girls were immediately placed into the care of the Saskatchewan Department of Social Services.

According to documents Jan has obtained, the department had "great difficulty" locating Mr. Sims "to determine if he was able to provide" for his daughters. Considering how particular the Immigration Branch was about checking a war bride's destination in Canada to ensure satisfactory arrangements, and knowing how frequently they turned down applicants when it became apparent that Canadian husbands could not provide for their families, it is difficult to understand how two little girls could have been transported halfway around the world and end up in a Regina foster home — at Christmas, no less.

It is known that Sims attended a court hearing on April 2, 1947, at which time the girls were deemed to have been "neglected" and were made wards of the department for twelve months. Two years later, at a court hearing held on June 10, 1949, Mr. Sims signed his daughters over to the permanent care of the province. That was the last time he had anything to do with his children.

What happened next is a story that is familiar to many foster children in this country. Jan and her sister were placed in a foster home in Regina, where Jan says they were physically and emotionally abused. Somehow the girls' names were changed to that of the foster family, even though they were not adopted, an insult which Jan recalls with bitterness even today. Jan left this home permanently at age fifteen, still a Crown ward. Under the authority of Social Services, a place was found for her to live on her own and living expenses were covered. Her sister Eileen stayed on with the foster family, and Jan lost contact with her. Jan is still looking for her today. All she knows is that Eileen has family in western Canada. Attempts to find Eileen through the authorities have been futile.

On one occasion, Jan came very close to finding a nephew, but bureaucratic red tape ensured the two would never meet. An attempt to locate her father in 1996 through Veterans Affairs resulted in a terse, two-paragraph letter telling her that her father was still alive but wanted nothing to do with his daughter:

> The Privacy Act protects personal information unless the person has been deceased for twenty years. We are not permitted to release personal information without personal authorization.

> Veterans Affairs have offered to convey your communica-
> tion to the above named individual. The individual expressed
> his preference to not receive such correspondence and we
> must respect this.

But Jan isn't the type to give up. In 2000, she heard about Olga and Lloyd Rains of Project Roots. Although the Rains deal primarily with so-called "illegitimate" children who were born of wartime unions between Canadian soldiers and British and European women, they are increasingly called upon to find the fathers of children whose parents married during the war. The details of Jan's case was different, but the questions were still the same: where was her father, and why did he abandon the two little girls so long ago?

The Rains put Jan's story up on their website, using her birth name, Philomena Sims. Even though the search story was repeatedly featured on the site's front page over the period of two years, nothing ever came of it. Then, in January 2002, the Rains discovered that Mr. Sims had passed away in October 2000. His last known address was the Brock Fahrni Pavilion in Vancouver. The Rains didn't know it at the time, but the date of death was wrong: Mr. Sims actually died five months later, in March 2001, a detail that led to some confusion with the British Columbia Public Trustee, who it was later determined had buried the old man when no one named in his will could be found to fulfill the terms of his estate.

In the meantime, Jan contacted the hospital's Release of Information Branch of the Health Record Services Department and made a formal request for information that would identify the next of kin on her father's death certificate.

One week later the hospital wrote back, but its answer was not what Jan wanted to hear:

> The registered next of kin from Mr. Sims' health record is
> that of a friend. In compliance with provincial legislation,
> we have contacted the next of kin for permission to give
> out their name and address. We are unable to assist you as
> this person wishes to remain anonymous but we wish you
> success in your endeavour.

Jan's immediate reaction was one of frustration and bitterness, but after some reflection she has decided to continue with her search. Having come so close, she doesn't want to give up now. With this story, she hopes that someone who knew her father, Clifford Harold Sims, will break the wall of silence that has shrouded her past since 1946. Perhaps the person named as next of kin, or someone who knows him or her, will come forward to help Jan understand why she and her sister were brought to Canada and abandoned by their father so long ago.

Postscript: Since this article was written in December 2002, Jan Walker has been reunited with her sister Eileen, who was found by Saskatchewan Post Adoption Services. Jan has also met her niece in Ontario and her nephew from western Canada. In January 2005, after much searching and with the help of Penny Denby, a researcher in Britain, Jan's brother, John Philip Sims, was finally located in Poole, England. Jan has spoken to John several times since finding him. He says he always knew he was adopted, but knew nothing about his parents, his sisters or the circumstances surrounding the girls' departure to Canada in December 1946.

In the spring of 2003, Lloyd and Olga Rains visited Jan's mother's grave at Portslade, England, where they took pictures for Jan. With the assistance of helpers in Vancouver, Jan also found her father's grave in Burnaby, British Columbia, but she still knows very little about his life before and after the war, other than that he was married at least once in Canada and may have fathered three boys.

Ironically, when contact was made with the British Columbia Trustee (the government agency that was responsible for burying Clifford Harold Sims and administering his estate), it was discovered that the two persons so named as beneficiaries in his will could not be located; therefore, as the oldest living child of Clifford Harold Sims, Jan was made the executor of her father's estate.

At first, it appeared that Jan might inherit what little her father left behind, but in the course of reinvestigating the whereabouts of the two persons named as beneficiaries in Mr. Sims' will, one person did finally come forward — Mr. Sims' second wife, who had been divorced from Jan's father for many years.

Incidentally, when Mr. Sims' ex-wife was first contacted by the trustee's office, the woman strangely refused to identify herself, gave a false name to the trustee and would not co-operate. The trustee persisted, however, and the woman presumably changed her mind when she found out there was some money in the estate. She laid claim to everything, including precious photographs and personal items that belonged to Jan's father. Jan got absolutely nothing, and nearly two years later, her father's former wife has made no attempt to contact Jan whatsoever. Jan doesn't care about the money, which she intended to distribute among her sister and niece. What bothers Jan most is the possibility that there may have been a photograph of her mother amongst her father's belongings. She will never know.

As for Jan's mother, Bridget Mary Sims, researcher Penny Denby tracked down a neighbour in Portslade who knew Bridget when she was pregnant with John Philip, but the man, who was just a child at the time, had little useful information to relate. Until someone comes forward who knows more about Bridget Mary Sims, she will remain an enigma and her grave in Portslade cemetery will be the only tangible evidence that she ever lived at all.

In June 2003, Jan Walker (left) and her sister Eileen met for the first time in 47 years at the Toronto airport.

Back Home to England
by Olga Rains

Diane's story begins in England in 1943, when her parents, Colleen and Mike, were married. The couple had a baby boy, and when the war was over plans were made for Colleen and the baby to immigrate to Canada. In March 1946, Colleen arrived at Pier 21 in Halifax on one of the war bride ships to start a new life in Canada.

Life in Canada wasn't always a dream come true for the war brides. In this photo, a young army wife shows off her new baby against the backdrop of PMQs on a Canadian army base.

Compared to other returning servicemen and their war brides, Colleen and Mike were lucky. That winter of 1946 was a cold one, with lots of snow, and they were able to rent an apartment on the second floor of a house. But the landlord did not keep their apartment very warm, and when Colleen complained, he told her that she should have stayed in England and married one of her own kind. So began Colleen's life in Canada.

She soon found out that her new in-laws weren't too thrilled at the prospect of an English daughter-in-law, and Mike's sister made it clear that Colleen had stolen her best friend's boyfriend. The woman had waited for Mike in the hope they would marry after he returned from the war.

Three months after Colleen came to Canada, their little son, then two years old, became very ill and died two months later. Colleen knew that she was pregnant again and both she and Mike were happy to have another child. But these were difficult times for the young couple: Colleen needed Mike's support, but he wasn't there for her. She was already on shaky ground with his family, and now they blamed her for the death of the boy. She wasn't a good mother, they said, and Mike wouldn't stand up to his parents. His way of avoiding conflict was to go to the Legion, where he stayed out drinking every night and spent what little money they had.

Colleen had long days alone. She had made some friends and had a small job to keep her busy until the baby came. A healthy little girl,

Diane, was born in 1947. In the meantime, Mike spent more and more time at the Legion and came home with less money every day. Colleen made up her mind to take Diane and go back to England as soon as she could save up for the fare. She couldn't live the life Mike wanted her to live: every other night at the Legion talking about the war, every Saturday night listening to the hockey game. Weekends were spent with the in-laws at the farm, where the insults about her British ways never stopped. Colleen took a full-time job and had a friend babysit Diane.After two years, she had enough money to return to England. "Just a visit," she told Mike, but she had no intention of returning to Canada. Colleen and Diane went back home to England.

Postscript: When Diane was old enough, she started looking for her father and found out that he had passed away when still young. Diane went to Canada once to visit her father's grave.

Husband in Jail
by Olga Rains

The majority of Canadian war brides arrived in Canada between February and December 1946, at Pier 21 in Halifax.

Lily and Roy met in Belgium during the closing months of the Second World War. They fell in love and decided to get married. It wasn't easy for a young soldier to get permission to marry during the war: paperwork had to be filled out, medical examinations taken and references obtained. Lily and Roy followed the rules and married after obtaining permission from his commanding officer.

By the time Roy was repatriated back to Canada, Lily was pregnant, and the letters she received from Roy from overseas were few and far between. He had promised Lily that he would get a job and a place to live in Canada as soon as possible, but months went by and she heard nothing from her husband.

The baby was born, a healthy little girl named Eloise. After that, Lily had only one letter from Roy saying that he wanted to move away from northern Ontario, where he was born and had lived most of his life.

As a war bride, Lily was entitled to free passage to Canada, so she went to the Canadian Wives Bureau in Brussels and told them her story. Following standard procedure, the Immigration Branch of the Department of Mines and Resources in Canada investigated her husband's situation in Ontario and gave their stamp of approval. They told Lily that she and the baby would be living with Roy's family in a small place called Geraldton, Ontario.

When the baby was three months old, Lily received a telegram advising her it was time to join her husband in Canada. Her parents begged her not to leave, but Lily was determined to make a go of her marriage. Besides, she had been assured by the Wives Bureau that everything was going to be fine, so she did not worry about what was waiting for her on the other side of the Atlantic.

After a very long journey by ship, train and bus, Lily and Eloise arrived in a small village in northern Ontario. She had hoped that Roy would be there, but for some reason he was not. At the train station, a little old lady, poorly dressed, came forward and introduced herself as

Roy's mother. What a meeting — both Lily and mother were crying, and so was little Eloise.

Lily's father-in-law was waiting outside in an old car and she was introduced to him. He worked in the bush and was rough-looking, but his eyes were kind as he looked at his Belgian daughter-in-law and little granddaughter.

After a long, rough drive along a remote bush path, they arrived at a log cabin where they were welcomed by a large, barking dog. An old truck was parked in the yard and Lily's first thoughts were that Roy was inside the cabin waiting to surprise his wife and daughter. She was just about to ask where he was when his mother handed her a letter:

> Dear Mrs. Lily B.
>
> I am obliged to give you the following information about your husband Roy B. He was convicted about a month ago to one year in jail for robbery. Roy B. is very restless, never holding a steady job. When the police picked him up he was with a woman who was supposed to be his wife.
>
> I am sure this information is heart breaking for you, but you have to know the truth. No doubt you found him an honest young man who you thought had honourable intentions towards you.
>
> After talking to his parents with whom you are staying, they offered to take you in for the time being. They asked us to wait to tell you this, until you had arrived at your destination.
>
> Sincerely
>
> Clerk at the Treasurer's Office

After reading this, Lily felt so very betrayed by everyone, from her husband to the Wives Bureau to Roy's parents. Why didn't they tell her this before she made the long journey to Canada? Her only thought was to return to Belgium as soon as possible.

Roy's mother hoped Lily would forgive Roy and wait for him to get out of jail. He needed her, and the war had been so hard on him. Lily stayed, and these people treated her the best they could, but she had no intention of living there any longer than necessary.

Lily visited Roy in jail a few times and talked to people in the village. She knew she could never be happy there. She looked around, saw their way of life and made up her mind to go back to Belgium. She became a member of the local church and found her strength there. Members of the parish helped her to get a job and looked after her baby while she worked. When she had enough money, she and little Eloise made the long journey back home to Belgium.

Eloise was now almost eighteen months old. Lily's parents took care of their granddaughter so that Lily could get a job and support the two of them. Life was hard for a while until she met Lorne, a nice young man who loved Lily and the baby. They dated for more than a year before he proposed, but Lily had to apply for a divorce because she was still married to Roy. Fortunately, this was not a problem because Roy had been in and out of jail, so Lily had grounds for divorce.

Lorne and Lily married, and Eloise grew up thinking that Lorne was her dad. Lily had two more children and they were a happy family. When Eloise was fifteen years old, someone in the family told her that her real father was a Canadian soldier. Eloise demanded to know the truth, and Lily told her as best she could about what happened after the war.

It wasn't until much later, when Eloise was married and had her first child, that she decided to trace her biological father in Canada. With the help of Project Roots she found out that her father had lived a very tumultuous life, in and out of jail, always drinking and getting into trouble with the law. At the age of forty-five, Roy had been killed in an automobile accident.

It was not the news Eloise wanted to hear, but at least she finally knew the truth about her Canadian father, Roy B.

I Thought He Was Going to Kill Me
by Olga Rains

Sally was an English war bride who struggled to make a life for herself in Canada, but her husband's alcoholism and abuse finally forced her back home. Like other war brides in similar circumstances, there was no help from the Canadian government and she had to finance her own journey to England.

Sally and Don married in England in 1943. The next year their first child, a girl, was born. Don was repatriated back to Canada shortly after the war ended, and she followed him seven months later with their baby daughter.

For a brief time they were a happy family, but as time passed Don became very nervous and aggressive. Nothing Sally did pleased him, and her British ways seemed to bother him. She soon realized that the man she was living with in Canada was not the same man she married in England.

She became pregnant again, and all during the pregnancy Don insulted her about the way she looked. He even hit her a few times, but Sally didn't tell anybody. She even covered up the blue marks on her body so that no one would know he was beating her.

Although Don was not a heavy drinker, after a few beers he turned into a wild man and would break things in the house. Sally had to hide to avoid his wrath. After their little boy, Wayne, was born, Don seemed to improve a bit, and at times he told Sally that he was sorry. He begged for forgiveness, and of course Sally forgave him because she still loved him very much, despite the abuse.

A year after Wayne was born they had another little boy who lived for only two days. Then the problems really started. Don blamed Sally for the baby's death and started hitting her again more often. Fearing he would kill her, Sally made a decision that probably saved her life.

She had saved some money, and with the help of another English war bride and her husband, Sally took the children and one suitcase, boarded the bus and kept going until she was far enough away that Don couldn't find her. She found some help from a group that assisted families in trouble and eventually made her way back to England.

Sally was able to get some work at home so that she could be with the children. At times life became very difficult because Wayne was a very nervous little boy and was often sick. She remarried a very compassionate man who was older than Sally and he loved the children as though they were his own. They are still together today.

As the years passed, Wayne's mental health deteriorated and he ended up in doctor's care. During this time, he decided to find his father in Canada, and he came into contact with Project Roots. We found Wayne's father in Canada, and the two have been in contact with each other by letter and phone. Since then, Wayne's health has improved, and even though Sally's memories of her Canadian marriage are not happy, she is glad that the reunion of father and son has had the unexpected benefit of improving Wayne's health. She is thankful to Project Roots for finding his father.

Really Desperate

The following is the text of a letter written to the Canadian Red Cross in March 1947.

Dear Sirs:

I'm writing to ask you if you could help me to go back to England. I've been in Canada a year on the 27th of this month. I have a boy 2 and a half years old also a baby six weeks. My husband has left me with $20 and my house rent is $20.00 per month. I have no money in the bank and I am really desperate. My husband sailed for England today from New York on the *Marine Marlin* and he says as soon as he arrives he'll get a job and send me my fare but I know that he'll not be able to do that for maybe a year because he has no money and that what he does earn he'll have to pay his board and send no money to live. So I wonder if you could please help to me to go back.

Yours truly,

Signed M.F.
Barriefield, Kingston

Chapter 4

War Children Who Were Adopted
by Melynda Jarratt

"Twice as much work to do."

In England, many war children were given up for adoption and put into the care of council-run orphanages. Winnie Bullen, pictured above, found these photos of herself in her file at London City Archives. The photos were taken every year as a marketing tool for prospective adoptive parents.

We will never know how many unwed mothers gave up their Canadian babies for adoption during World War II, but it is likely in the thousands. That so many women would choose adoption should come as no surprise; not only was there no safety net for unwed mothers, but social attitudes and the stigma of bearing an illegitimate child made the prospect of adoption the only way out for many desperate women.

War children who were adopted have twice as much work to do: not only do they have to find their Canadian fathers, but they have to find their mothers, too. The difficulty this presents, even for an experienced investigator, can be overwhelming. Leads that go nowhere, and twice as many parents to be found — in two different countries — can make a search frustrating and depressing. But most keep looking, and when they do find their parents they can put the past behind them and look forward to the future, no matter what it may bring.

Adoption societies in England such as the Catholic Children's Society and the Church of England Children's Society (formerly known as the Waifs and Strays Society) kept excellent records of the children in their care and, as we will see in this chapter, it is possible to obtain access to files if one is so determined. Those who have the wherewithal to fill out the extensive paperwork, and the financial resources to pay the fees that are often associated with a detailed search, can be rewarded with the identity of their biological parents.

But knowing the names of one's parents and actually finding them are two different things: war children still have a lot of work to do before a meeting can take place. First and foremost, they have to find out if their parents are still alive, and in order to do that, they must ascertain where these men and women live today. Given the passage of time since the children were born, parents have likely moved on — addresses from the 1940s are no longer valid. And even if the last known address of a parent can be tracked down, the sad fact in many cases is that there is nobody alive who remembers the mother or father when they lived at that address.

In this regard, adoptees are in the same position as war children who were lucky enough to be raised by their mothers and who know the name and address of a Canadian father but cannot locate him because the address is no longer valid. They, too, are prevented by Canada's Privacy Act from obtaining any information about his present location that may reside in his military personnel file at the National Archives in Ottawa. (For further discussion on this issue, please read Chapter 8.)

Finding a mother in Britain, Holland or Belgium is the first step in the process, and if a war child can find her, then it is possible to find the Canadian father as well. That is precisely what has happened in many of the cases described in this chapter. Mothers are located through the well-kept, and accessible, British, Dutch and Belgian adoption records of the period.

Once contact is made, and if the mother is co-operative, the next step is to find the father in Canada. With as little to go on as a photograph, a last name or a regimental number, many adopted war children have found their fathers in Canada with the help of the birth mothers who willingly share the information.

But just because a mother has been found doesn't guarantee a happy reunion. As many war children find out, not all birth mothers are happy to be found after so many years and they definitely aren't forth-coming. The war, their relationship with the father, their pregnancy and all the bad memories it dredges up are something their birth mothers would rather forget and no amount of pleading for his name will change their minds.

These situations are always heartbreaking, because the war child has to accept that the only person in the entire world who can identify his or her father refuses to help, or worse, deliberately misleads, taking their secret to the grave.

Another major factor that impedes adoptee war children is a sense of obligation to their adoptive parents. Torn between a duty to the loving parents who brought them up and a search for their biological parents, they frequently choose to wait until their adoptive parents are dead before starting the process. Still others only find out they were adopted after their parents have died and they stumble upon papers they were never meant to see.

No matter what the circumstances, the situation facing adoptee war children is the most complicated and difficult to solve. Project Roots has been involved with many such cases, and as the men and women in this chapter show, the road to finding a long-lost mother and father from World War II is a difficult one indeed.

My Dad Was Killed in France
by Pamela Walker

My name is Pamela Walker and I was born in Huddersfield, West Yorkshire, England. My birth mother, Grace, is English and my father was a Canadian soldier named Robert Cecil Martin from Nova Scotia.

My mother was already married with two children when she became pregnant with me. Her husband, understandably, would not take her back if she kept me, so three weeks after I was born on February 27, 1945, I was adopted. My new family never spoke about my adoption, but I knew from a very early age that circumstances did not add up.

My parents were strict, but I had a good upbringing. As I grew older I wanted to know who my biological parents were. While searching for my birth mother I came in contact with her first-born, a son by the name of Arthur Benstead. My half-brother became the mediator between my mother and me. Arthur spoke to our mother about what happened during the war and she slowly opened up and told him the story.

Grace told Arthur that my father was a Canadian soldier named Robert Martin. Robert was a craftsman with the 4th Armoured Troops Workshop, a unit of the Royal Canadian Electrical and Mechanical Engineers. Grace did not know for sure why he did not come back for her, but when the letters stopped she guessed he had been killed. Her memory was vague on details, but she remembered

Robert Cecil Martin was killed in the invasion of Normandy on August 4, 1944, and his pregnant girlfriend never knew what happened to him.

Robert having his twenty-second birthday party before he left for Normandy. His birthday was July 2. Within a month he was dead, killed in action in Normandy on August 4, 1944.

I contacted the Ministry of Defence in London and they suggested I write to the Canadian Historical Museum in Ottawa. I also wrote to a number of addresses in England, but none of them could give me the information that I needed.

One evening I was listening to the radio and a program came on called *The McDavids Reunion Song*. It was about people in the same situation who were trying to trace their biological fathers. I was amazed that there were so many in the same circumstances. I wrote to the BBC reporters who researched the programme and they sent me Lloyd and Olga Rains' address.

I contacted the Rains with what little information that I had. They told me that Robert Martin was a common name in Canada, and the search would be more difficult because I did not know from which part of the country he came. After a long search, a few years later Project Roots had a lead. Unfortunately it lead to the Commonwealth War Graves, where they found the name Robert Cecil Martin in the Beny-Sur-Mer Canadian Cemetery in Reviers, Calvados. In this cemetery are the graves of Canadians who gave their lives in the Normandy landings and in the earlier stages of the subsequent campaign in France. There they found my dad's grave, and on it the inscription, "Robert Cecil Martin, Son of John Saunders Martin and Mavis G. Martin, Gabarouse, Nova Scotia." He was killed in action on August 4, 1944, when he was twenty-two years old.

With that little bit of information, Project Roots searched in the village of Gabarouse, Cape Breton, Nova Scotia, but there were no Martins. By dialling a number at random they spoke to a man named Daniel MacIntyre. He said he had gone to the same school as Robert Martin and knew where some of the family lived. He gave the telephone number of Irene, one of Robert's sisters.

Olga rang Irene and told her about me. She was very surprised; no one knew that he had fathered a child while in England. One older sister knew that he had a girlfriend, as he had mentioned this to her in a letter. I contacted Irene and asked for a photo of Robert, which she sent. When I received the photo, I could see the resemblance.

The next step was to let my biological mother, Grace, see the photo to confirm whether this really was my dad. Arthur took the photo, and Grace recognized Robert Martin right away. She also remembered that he had a middle name — Cecil — and that he came from a large family, thirteen in all!

Some of my dad's brothers and sisters have died, but I correspond regularly with three of my aunts, who live in various parts of Canada. They accepted that I was part of their family straightaway. I am also in touch with a lady who has looked after my father's grave, and I hope to travel to France one day to see her and visit the cemetery.

Postscript: After Pamela made contact with her Canadian family, she wrote Project Roots:

Dear Olga:

Here is a photo of my dad. Yes, my dad! Isn't he good-looking! My birth mother recognised him right away when Arthur showed her the photo. My family in Canada have been wonderful. We have written so many letters already. Someday I hope I can visit them and meet them all of my Canadian family. I look very much like my dad. Aunt Irene has sent me photos of my grandparents. I hope to visit my dad's grave very soon. I realise now what a difficult time my birth mother must have had, not knowing where Robert was or that he was killed. I am very grateful for Project Roots and for my half-brother Arthur Benstead for all the help they gave me to find my Canadian family.

A Wonderful Surprise
by Irene Lynk

When I received a phone from Holland telling me that my brother, the late Robert Cecil Martin, had left behind a war baby in England, I thought it was a cruel joke. You see, my brother was killed in France on August 4, 1944.

Robert was a brother I really did not know. We come from a family of thirteen children — seven girls and six boys. I was the little sister, only four years old when Robert went off to war, and I was only eight when he was killed. I only wish I could see him today!

My mother and father took the news of Robert's death very hard. Robert was their second-oldest child and was much loved.

So when the woman on the other end of the telephone, Olga Rains, told me that Robert had a beautiful daughter in England. I was shocked, to say the least. She told me Pamela Walker was my late brother's child, born on February 27, 1945.

Pamela Walker in a recent photo. Pamela's aunt, Irene Lynk, calls her a "wonderful surprise."

I just couldn't believe it at first, and I wondered how Olga had found me. I am married, so I do not use the Martin name, and our family moved from that village in Cape Breton, so there aren't any Martins in the telephone book anymore. As Olga explained, she randomly picked a Scottish name out of the Cape Breton telephone book and crossed her fingers that someone might know the late Robert Cecil Martin. She hit the jackpot on the first call.

Daniel MacIntyre knew Robert because they went to school together and he knew where our family had moved to so long ago. Daniel gave Olga my married name and the name of the place I now live: Big Ridge, Nova Scotia.

Olga told me that Pamela would call. A few days later, when the phone rang and I heard Pamela's voice, I broke down and cried. I gave the phone to Darlene, my daughter, so she could take over the conversation until I stopped crying. The tears streamed down my face during the entire conversation I had with Pamela. She kept asking me, "Are you okay?"

Pamela is a wonderful surprise for our whole family and everyone loves her. I know that my parents would have loved her, too. We have written lots of letters and exchanged photos, and we call each other often and talk. I hope that someday Pamela will visit us here in Canada and meet all of her Canadian family.

I sincerely thank Project Roots for doing this — for bringing into my life a niece I never knew I had.

Dear John
by Margaret Atkinson

My name is Margaret Atkinson. I was born in England at the end of April 1945. My mother was Mary Wetherell, a chemical worker, and my father was a Canadian airman with the RCAF in Leeming, Yorkshire. I do not know his name, so I am going to call him John.

Dear John:

I don't know your real name, which is the reason for my writing this open letter. Perhaps I should start at the beginning:

How well do you remember being stationed at Leeming, Yorkshire, in late 1944?

My research tells me that you were most likely an airgunner (WAG) with either 429 or 427 Squadron, Royal Canadian Air Force (RCAF). Both squadrons were based at Leeming at that time.

If you were with 429, I will almost certainly have your name on my list of some 200 air gunners, helpfully supplied by Greg Kopchuk of Edmonton, who has been invaluable in providing me with details.

Back in 1944, you were dating a Miss Mary Wetherell, a 19- or 20-year-old chemical worker from Thornaby or Stockton-on-Tees.

Mary Wetherhall, Margaret Atkinson's biological mother, in her wedding photo, which was taken a few years after she gave up her baby for adoption.

You will already have noticed the picture of Mary, included with this letter, and hopefully, you will have recognized her. The photograph was taken three or four years after you knew her, but her striking appearance is quite clear. I believe that you were dating Mary for several months in late 1944, but that the relationship ended abruptly.

In fact, the relationship ended when Mary made the 40-mile trip along with a girlfriend to Leeming to give you the news that you were to be a father — my father!

When the two women reached the airbase, I understand that they saw you in the distance, across the parade ground. However, in order to talk to you, they had to get clearance from the squadron commander. He asked the purpose of the visit and when he found out, he gave Mary the sad news that you were married, with a wife back in Canada. I think it quite likely that that was a stock answer given to all women who found themselves in such an unfortunate predicament, and probably was not true.

Mary and her friend left the base at once, out of your life for good and so suddenly.

Margaret Atkinson was given up for adoption at birth. She is still looking for her Canadian father.

At the end of April 1945, I was born. I was very soon adopted by my "real" parents, with whom I had an extremely happy upbringing and life.

I was married in the 1960s, and we have a son and a daughter, both now graduates. So you see, John, you started a small dynasty and probably didn't even suspect it.

Even if you, reading this letter, are not John but you were also stationed in Leeming in 1944 and remember the girl in the photo, I would be delighted to hear from you also.

My reasons for pursuing this are first to solve a family mystery and second, to make John aware of the course of events after Mary disappeared from his life. Incidentally Mary is no longer alive. I never met her. Indeed, until two years ago I didn't know anything about her and no one else remembers your name.

Making contact with you will not produce any recriminations on my part. I give you this written assurance that I am trying to find out who you are for only the best of motives and to satisfy my long-held curiosity.

I look forward to having some positive response to my letter in due course, from you John, and/or from any others with any light to shed on the situation.

Margaret Atkinson

Foundling
by Melynda Jarratt

Winnie Bullen presents one of the most difficult cases Project Roots has ever seen. A foundling, Winnie knows absolutely nothing about her mother or her father. She was abandoned in a telephone kiosk in the Strand, West London, on February 21, 1945. As she carried no identification, doctors assessed her age as two months and assigned her an arbitrary birth date of December 21, 1944. Since the nurse who found her was named Winifred Anne, and she was found near Bowe Street police station in West London, the infant was named Winifred Anne West by the child welfare authorities.

Winnie Bullen as a cute little five-year-old. Child welfare authorities had a hard time placing Winnie because of her rebellious behaviour.

From there, Winnie was placed in the Chelsea Institution for orphans, and for the next seven years her life was a succession of orphanages and failed foster homes. She was finally adopted at age seven by an English couple and given the last name Moncrieff. Winnie recalls that her life was not a bed of roses with the Moncrieffs, who she believes should never have been allowed to adopt. In their application form, the father cites his leadership in the Boy Scouts and includes recommendations from acquaintances who don't seem to know the couple very well. According to Winnie, her father was very controlling and her mother submissive, but for the first time, the little girl stayed put. As a young adult, she married, and together she and her husband immigrated to Canada, settling in Bathurst, New Brunswick.

In the early 1980s, Winnie's parents followed her to Bathurst, settling nearby, but it was never a good relationship and the move did not make matters any better. Winnie had never seen eye-to-eye with her father, and she felt that he moved to Canada because he couldn't control her from England. She resisted and, as always, there was a simmering tension between the two.

Eventually, Winnie and her husband divorced and Winnie went her own way. She moved to Fredericton and took a BA in religious studies at St. Thomas University. Along with her spiritual awakening came a newfound determination to make some sense of her early years. In April 1999, after reading an article about Project Roots in the New Brunswick *Telegraph-Journal*, Winnie contacted Project Roots and we put her story on the website in faint hope she might find her biological parents. In six years, we have not had a single lead, but now that both her adoptive parents have passed away, Winnie feels free to pursue her search and allow us to include details of her adoption file in this book.

Much of what Winnie knows about her early years was found in the files of the London City Council's Social Welfare Department. In her record is the story of a very unhappy little girl who for some reason was not adopted as an infant and remained in orphanages until age seven. It is surprising that such a cute little girl was not adopted for so long, as there certainly was a market for babies and even toddlers. But in looking at her records, it probably had more to do with her questionable heritage and the fear that she might not be suitable for adoption in a "good," middle-class home.

Even at two years of age, the social workers had decided that Winnie came from a lower-class background, and that that was where she belonged. On January 11, 1947, her social worker, Miss Siddel, recommended Winnie for adoption to "a working class home, as she is rather on the tough side, a real little East Ender." How the social worker could make such an assessment with no information to base it on is just one of many baffling statements scattered throughout her file.

But the plan to send Winnie to a working-class family never transpired. For some reason, Miss Siddel's superiors overruled her and Winnie was instead transferred from the orphanage to foster care, called "boarding." As the files show, between the ages of four and seven, Winnie spent a lot of time travelling back and forth between the orphanage and new foster homes. The goal, of course, would be for Winnie to be adopted, but as the records show, at least five separate foster mothers tried to take Winnie on, with abject failure. It did not help that even when people tried to be nice to her, Winnie deliberately sabotaged relationships and potential adoptions by acting out in the most unladylike manner, getting herself kicked out of one home after another for her tantrums.

On May 11, 1948, when Winnie was four, Miss Siddel reported that another of Winnie's foster mothers, a Mrs. Harmon, said she could not keep Winnie any longer.

> She is upset and disappointed by her apparent failure with Winnie. The child behaved quite well at first and then became restless and had temper tantrums. She would scream and lie on the floor and kick if she couldn't get her own way. This often happened when she was out too. This screaming upset the people in the flat below.

Mrs. Harmon said that Winnie had a very independent nature and was not affectionate. She felt she would do better on a farm where there were other children.

> I still think as I said in my previous reports that the rough and tumble of a working class home would be best for Winnie. She has greatly improved in appearance of late. She is much slimmer and her hair is growing. She looks almost pretty at times. Holly Shaw (orphanage) reports that she seemed delighted to be back with the other children and seemed to have missed their company.
> Miss Siddel 8/5/48

Winnie admits she was a "hellion," but she says there are reasons why. "In the orphanage, you had to protect yourself from the older boys, some of whom were as old as age eighteen, so I used to hide in the closet to get away from them. I don't have to tell you what they did to us girls."

Winnie is still afraid of dogs, a fear cultivated at the orphanage, which used a vicious dog to frighten the children into their beds at night.

In this excerpt from a letter written on April 21, 1949, another foster mother, a Mrs. Hearns, wrote to the social worker:

> Dear Sir:
>
> Winifred West has been living with us for about five months, but I regret to say we must send her away. I have a little boy of nearly five years whom I adopted 2 yrs ago and thought Winifred would be a companion to him, but it has not worked out as I had expected.

When Winnie first came here she told lies as a matter of course, she does not do this nearly so often now, but she is a very determined child and sometimes if she has her mind set on something or wants to do anything she shouldn't she will do it at all costs. This trait, as you can imagine, has put us to considerable trouble, but we persevered with her and recently thought she was alright but in one day she broke a part of the vacuum cleaner and put the brake up in the car causing it to run backwards...

In June 1950, Winnie was fostered out to a Mrs. Wraight, and in what becomes a depressing pattern throughout her file, Winnie brought along with her a detailed list, titled, "List of clothing and personal possessions brought by Winifred Anne West":

1 hair brush, 1 comb, 1 toothbrush, 1 pair Wellingtons, 1 rain hat and coat, 2 winter boots, 1 summer coat, 3 Cardigans, 3 pair shoes, 1 pair rubber shoes, 1 pair slippers, 1 dress gown, 3 night dress, 1 pair sandals, 1 mac and hat, 10 dresses 7 summer 3 winter, 1 kilt and 5 skirts, 6 blouses, 1 sunsuit, 2 liberty bodices, 6 vests 2 winter 4 summer, 9 pairs of knickers, 7 socks, 4 handkerchiefs, 4 woolen jumpers, 1 sunhat, 7 aprons.

In February 1951, six-year-old Winnie was back at Mrs. Hearns's, but the foster mother was ready to send her back again because "I am almost at my wits end with Winnie."

We told her yesterday that we would have to see you and tell you how naughty she was. She just turned round, laughed this is just what she said. "I will take all my toys to a new house but Rita [the foster parent's other child] can't come." I can't imagine why or what possessed her to say it ... believe me, I have tried earnestly to make Winnie happy and feel she is loved by us all, but it just doesn't seem to work out, she can so easily cry when she wants sympathy and that seems to get her by.... Yesterday she was brought back from Sunday School kicking and screaming, she was so naughty Edna had to bring her home.

Soon after, Winnie was brought back to the home where Mr. Wheeler, inspector of child care, personally investigated her case after complaints about her behaviour "in each of the foster homes to which she has been sent during the past two years or so." Mr. Wheeler noted that the main complaints were "day and night wetting, morbid thirst, jealousy and destructiveness, particularly regarding clothes."

> It is difficult to describe the kind of home to look for but it is one in which the foster parents are really mature, kindly and understanding and yet firm. I do not think it would be wise to choose a home where there are children younger than Winnie though she might be able to settle where there are one or more older children so that she is not too much the centre of attraction and yet has a fairly privileged position. It would be unwise to saddle too young a couple with her problems, nevertheless, elderly candidates should be examined with care.
> Mr. Wheeler, Inspector of Child care.

Into the picture entered the Moncrieffs, who must have seemed a godsend to the frustrated social workers in charge of Winnie. On November 2, 1953, the adoption was finalized and thereafter, the little foundling became Winnie Ann Moncrieff.

Winnie Bullen in a recent photo.

Winnie always presumed that it would be useless to even attempt to track down her birth parents, but since so many people like her have been successful through Project Roots, she has decided to give it a try.

The timing is right for her mother to have been a single, unwed British woman and her father a Canadian or other Allied soldier. That year, thousands of illegitimate children were born in Britain. Like so many other children born in late 1944 or early 1945, Winnie would have been conceived in the months leading up to D-Day, when hundreds of thousands of Allied soldiers prepared for the murderous onslaught on the beaches of Normandy.

Given the circumstances, Winnie certainly would not have been the only abandoned child during the war years, as the shame of being pregnant out of wedlock would have forced her mother to desperate measures. Perhaps her father had been killed in northwestern Europe after D-Day and her mother could not bear raising a child alone? Only one person has the key to Winnie's past — the young woman who gave her up that cold day in February 1945.

Life Is So Different for Me Now
by Peter

My name is Peter, and I was born in Holland near the Belgian border. My mother was a sixteen-year-old girl named Dina and my father was a Canadian soldier named Eddie Murray.

The southern part of Holland was liberated in the fall of 1944 by the Allies, mostly Canadians, who stayed in the area until the spring of 1945. That winter, many girls became pregnant by Canadian soldiers, and these babies were all born in 1945. I was one of them.

Dina met Eddie Murray that fall, after his regiment liberated the small village in southern Holland where she lived. The Canadian soldiers were due for a rest period, so they fraternized with people in the village who were most happy to make the Canadian soldiers welcome.

They met at a dance and dated for almost two weeks. The soldiers moved on to Germany to the fighting lines. Eddie wrote to Dina a few weeks later, but her English was not good, so she asked a friend to translate it. Eddie asked Dina to marry him when the war was over and she answered "yes" in her broken English.

A month later, Dina knew for sure that she was pregnant. She wrote Eddie, but he never replied. Dina's parents were very upset. They went to the Catholic Church for help, and my mother was put in a home for unwed mothers until I was born. In those days, most people in the area obeyed the church in every way: after all, my mother had sinned and had to pay a price.

Dina died in childbirth. My grandparents did not want me and I was put into an orphanage. I had no mother and no father, and the family did not want me, so I stayed there until I was sixteen years old.

As I grew older, I wanted to know who my parents were, so I asked if there were any records at the home. They told me that there were some files, but they had gone to another office. That is all they would tell me at the time.

On my sixteenth birthday I left the home and there I was, alone in the world. Soon I found a job on a boat. It was hard work, but I enjoyed it. As the years passed by I decided to find out more about my parents. When I was twenty-five, I placed an ad in a newspaper in the village where I knew my mother had lived.

To my surprise, I received one letter and it was from an old friend of my mother, Corrie, the lady who had translated the letter from my father twenty-five years earlier. I went to see her, and we had a long talk.

She told me that my father was a Canadian soldier who fought in World War II. She even remembered his name as being Eddie! She wasn't sure of the last name, but she knew it sounded like "murri."

Now I knew who my mother was and even saw her photo! With this information I went back to the home and asked them for help. The records were kept in The Hague and I had to make an appointment to view them, which I did right away.

The old lady was right about my father's name. On the birth certificate was his name and regiment. With this new information I started searching for him in Canada, but it was not meant to be. Every office I wrote to turned me down, citing Canada's Privacy Act as the reason they could not release any information until he was dead for twenty years. I could not believe it!

So I found another way. I searched through telephone books and libraries and sent letters to 1,500 people by the name Murray. I received a few answers back, but not the right one. After more searching I found the address of my father's regiment. I wrote to them with my story in the hope that they could give me help as to where my father came from in Canada. They answered in a few lines, saying they had never heard my father's name. Later, in Canada, I met one of my father's comrades, who told me that they didn't want to say anything about him because the old soldiers are loyal to each other.

Since Peter (centre) met his Canadian family in Cape Breton, his life has never been the same.

Some years went by, and I didn't get anywhere with the search for my Canadian father. Then I read an article about Project Roots in the newspaper and I decided to ask them for help.

It wasn't long before Lloyd and Olga Rains knew what part of Canada the regiment came from. They started searching in that province, and soon they were in touch with my half-brother, John, who was very surprised that he had a half-brother in Holland.

Apparently, my father told his family about a Dutch girl he dated during the war. After Holland, he went on to Germany, where he lost his leg in battle. He was shipped back to Canada, where his life took a different turn. He did not want to get married and remained single until he met Joan, a Canadian girl. They had two boys and a girl. Eddie died in 1980, never knowing he had a son in Holland.

After a few letters and phone calls back and forth, I went to Canada in 1996 to meet my Canadian family. What a wonderful feeling to belong to a family. One of my half-brothers and I look very much alike. Janet, my half-sister, is a lovely lady and can't do enough for me. She even made up an album for me with photos of my grandparents, aunts and uncles, nieces and nephews.

Life is so different for me now. After meeting my Canadian family I know that I am not alone in the world anymore!

Still Looking
by Olga Rains

Kathleen Swann was born on March 5, 1946, in Northumberland, England, and immediately given up for adoption. She was reunited with her mother in 1977, but asking about her father caused a rift between the two and they've never reconciled.

Kathleen has little to go on, except bits of information gleaned from sympathetic relatives on her mother's side. It's been a particularly difficult search because Kathleen's mother was determined that he never be found — refusing to identify him at first, and then deliberately misleading her daughter with the wrong name.

"The photograph on this page is the only one I have. My mother gave it to me quite freely, but with the wrong name," Kathleen explained.

It was only after an extensive search at Canada's National Archives in Ottawa that Kathleen determined there was no such soldier. Now she's starting to wonder about a lot of things she's been told about her father, like the horrifying story of his death.

"I was told that my father was killed clearing mines from the beaches in France after D-Day in 1944, that he was decapitated, his head sent home to his mother and his body buried in France." She was also told that he had no other relatives than his aged mother in Canada. Since then, she's been able to gather little snippets of information from her mother's family.

"He was called Robert," Kathleen says, "was known as Bob, and he drove tanks. He entertained his army buddies with his singing voice and he was a very nice person."

Kathleen figures he would have been born in 1920, making him about twenty-five years old in 1945–46.

Kathleen Swann has never met her father, but she thinks fondly of him every day. This is the only picture she has of her father. All she knows is that his name is Robert.

You're My Hero
by Melynda Jarratt

William "Willy" Joorman was born to an unwed, single mother in an Arnhem convent on June 20, 1946. His mother was forced by her parents into a home for unwed mothers, and like many of the 6,000 war children born in the year following the Canadian liberation of Holland, William was given up for adoption.

The adoption was illegal. On June 21 — the day after he was born — William was simply taken from his teenaged mother and given to new parents who drew up their own birth certificate for the new baby. William was renamed Tommy after his adoptive father, and he grew up believing he was theirs.

Yvon Pelletier in a wartime photo. Yvon had no idea that his Dutch girlfriend was pregnant because he never received the letters she sent him after the war.

Life was not easy for William. His parents were very businesslike and cold. Although he had everything a boy could ever want, he felt different from children his age. William was seventeen years old before he stumbled upon the truth about his birth, and the shock was so great that it sent him reeling into a path of self-destruction from which he is only now emerging.

At first, William thought that his father was a German soldier, and he begged his parents to tell him the truth. From them he learned that his real father was a Canadian soldier and that his mother was a Dutch teenager who became pregnant after the Liberation in 1945. William was relieved in a way, but now he wanted to find his biological parents. Where could he start?

With the little bit of information provided by his adoptive parents, William went to the social welfare office and asked for help. He talked to a sympathetic social worker who promised she would do all she could for him. The worker contacted William's mother, but the news was not what he wanted to hear.

"Your mother is a pretty blonde lady and she cried when she heard that you are looking for her," the social worker said. But William's mother did not want to see him, at least not until he was married and had children of his own. The news was difficult for William to accept. His mother was the only one who could tell him about his father and answer the many questions he had about his birth. William gave up hoping she would change her mind. He tried to forget about the past, he landed a good job and met a nice woman and they got married.

But William could not forget. He started drinking to dull the pain, and his wife, fed up with his boozing, eventually walked out on him. He cleaned up his act and a few years later, he remarried. After his second child was born he went back to the same social worker and reminded her of his mother's promise to see him once he had children of his own.

The social worker went to William's mother with the new information about his family, but in the years since his first inquiry, she had changed her mind and didn't want to meet him anymore.

It was a devastating blow that struck to the very core of William's identity. He crawled back into the bottle, and every attempt to stop drinking ended in failure. Although his wife was sympathetic, she could not stand William's drinking anymore. She took the children and left William, threatening to never return.

The shock of losing his family finally knocked some sense into William. He stopped drinking, and his wife and children came back to live with him in a final attempt to save their marriage.

In 1981, with their third child just born, William decided to find his mother one last time. He went back to the city hall in Arnhem and found a clerk who was willing to listen to his story. The man left the small waiting room for a few moments, and when he returned he had William's file. Without any hesitation whatsoever, he gave William the name and address of his real mother. William could not believe it!

He rushed to the address, but there was nobody home, so he left a note in the hope that his mother would contact him. Nothing happened for several days. Then one evening, the doorbell rang. Standing at the door was the husband of William's birth mother.

"Your mother is in the car," the man said.

Thirty-five years after she had given him up for adoption, William watched his birth mother emerge from the car and walk slowly towards him. William could not move, he was frozen to the ground. They fell into each other's arms and cried, looking at each other and holding hands — just standing there, saying nothing. It was an emotional reunion for both of them.

The war years had had a profound impact on his mother's life, and she was reluctant to become too attached to her newfound son. She eventually did break down and told William his father was a French-Canadian soldier named Yvon Pelletier, that he was from New Brunswick, and that she had been in love with him. She said William looked very much like his father.

She explained that her parents had been against the relationship because she was a teenager and they thought she was too young. Like many Dutch parents, they were afraid of losing their daughter to a Canadian soldier — as was happening to so many young women who married and left Holland for a new life in Canada. When she became pregnant, they forced her into a convent, where she had the baby; and then, a day later, they gave the infant away. She was not allowed to leave the convent until 1949, a real-life prisoner of wartime circumstances.

William's mother had written many letters to Yvon Pelletier in Canada, but she was unaware that the letters she wrote from the convent were intercepted by the nuns, who destroyed them. When she left the convent in 1949, she continued to write to Yvon, but he never responded. Little did she know that his mother in Canada was also destroying the letters. She finally faced reality and stopped writing in 1951.

William and his birth mother were not destined to spend much time together. Four months later, she told him she did not want to see him again. He tried hard to keep the relationship going, but it was too difficult for her psychologically, and even though it hurt him terribly to be rejected again, he understood her reasons; and besides, she had given him so much — his father's name!

William never saw his mother again. She died recently.

With the few clues provided by his mother, William set about looking for Yvon Pelletier, but it was not easy. He already knew that the Canadian authorities would not help; he had written to the Department of Veteran's Affairs and the Records Centre at the National Archives in Ottawa and got absolutely nowhere.

The people at the records centre explained that the provisions of the Canadian Privacy Act prevented them from releasing information about veterans to anyone but immediate relatives until at least twenty years after the person has passed away. There were no exceptions, especially for the war children of World War II: according to the strict definition of the term, they were not considered legitimate children of the Canadian veterans.

In 1985, William was put in contact with Project Roots. He gave Lloyd and Olga Rains all the information he had and the Rains started their search. But no matter how hard they tried, they could not seem to find Yvon Pelletier.

Every dead end drove William crazy with frustration. Did he have brothers or sisters? Were they looking for him? He had read a story about a family like his in one of the big Dutch newspapers. On his deathbed, a Canadian veteran told his daughter that he had a son in Holland. He gave her the name and city and she tracked down her half-brother for a happy reunion. Why couldn't that happen to him?

Once again, William took up the bottle to cope with his problems. He lost his job, and this time, his wife left him for good, taking their three children with her. With no job or family attachments keeping him tied down in Holland, William became a drifter and ended up in Eastern Europe, where he spent some time after the fall of the Berlin Wall.

When he finally came back to Holland, William started to look for his father again. Thinking Yvon Pelletier may have been killed in Holland during the war, he confined his search to the well-tended Canadian cemeteries scattered throughout the Dutch countryside.

In one of the graveyards, he found a white cross marker with the name of Joseph Pelletier on it. Pelletier had been killed in action, and William wondered if this might be his father. Maybe his mother had given him the wrong name?

William spent many nights at the grave, crying and drinking, a bottle of vodka by his side. He was certain that Joseph Pelletier was his father. William was at the lowest point in his life, and he knew it. He sought professional help for his serious drinking problems, and in the course of his recuperation, he met his third wife, Cynthia, whom he married in 1995. Once again, William's life was looking up.

In 1997, after twelve years of searching, Olga and Lloyd Rains found Yvon Pelletier's family in Lac Baker, New Brunswick. With the assistance of a person who shall forever remain unnamed, the Rains were able to ascertain that the Yvon Pelletier who William said was his father was the same one who had lived and worked his entire life in Lac Baker.

When Pelletier died in 1961, he left behind a devoted wife, three daughters and two sons — all of whom seemed interested in meeting their new brother William. In May 1998, William's wish to meet his real family came true. Four of the five Pelletier siblings took a secret, all-expenses-paid trip to Holland, where they were reunited with their half-brother on a live Dutch television show called *You're My Hero*.

William thought he was appearing on the show to thank Olga and Lloyd for finding his Canadian father, but it was all a ruse. The show's producers had actually arranged for the Pelletier brothers and sisters to fly over from Canada to surprise William.

When the four Pelletier siblings walked out onto the stage, William threw up his hands to his face and cried, "It's a miracle!" The brothers and sisters hugged each other and cried in front of the audience, many of whom had tears in their eyes as well.

After spending a few days together in Holland, William's brothers and sisters returned to Canada, but they keep in touch with William by telephone and letters. Someday, he hopes to go to Lac Baker to see the places where his father grew up and to meet the rest of his Canadian family.

The New Brunswick family meets Willy Joorman for the first time on Dutch television. Left to right: Odette, Roseline and Gilles Pelletier, Willy Joorman and Lise Pelletier.

Postscript: Willy Joorman never got a chance to come to Canada. He passed away in 2002, leaving behind his wife, Cynthia, and a new baby. Before he died, he wrote an autobiography called *The Left Behind*, in which he described the story of his search for his father.

Chapter 5

Native Roots
by Melynda Jarratt

"Our ancestry can never be denied."

Native soldiers also had relationships with the women they met overseas, and many of them had babies. In this photo are Willy Van Ee's Dutch mother and his Native Canadian father, Walter Mejaki, from the Sagamok Anishnawbek Band of Manitoulin Island in Ontario.

Like other Canadian soldiers, Native Canadians[1] had relationships with the British and European women they met overseas during World War II. The babies they left behind were different from those born of parents with strictly British or European roots: they had almost Asiatic features, with dark skin and eyes, and they stood out from other children their age. In many cases, the children didn't even know if their Canadian roots were Italian, Japanese or Chinese. It never occurred to them that their fathers could be Native.

More than 3,000 Native Canadians joined the Canadian army, air force and navy during World War II. The numbers would probably have been higher if not for systemic racism within the Royal Canadian Navy and Air Force which made it difficult, if not impossible, for Natives to join during the first three years of the war. The Navy, for example, required each recruit to be a "British born subject of White Race," and the Air Force restricted entrance to recruits of "pure European descent."[2] According to Janice Summersby, author of *Native Soldiers: Foreign Battlefields*, the exact number of Native veterans may never be known:

> "...the actual number of Native recruits is likely higher than the figure recorded since ... some Indians and most Metis and Inuit were excluded from Indian Affairs' tally. As well, it is not known how many served of the Natives who at that time no longer held Indian Status. Furthermore, an unknown number of Canadian Indians from reserves near the Canada-United States border served with the American forces."[3]

Native men walked off the reserves and became part of the Canadian military, where they endured culture shock, racism and discrimination. They served in every major battle and campaign, including Dieppe, Normandy and Hong Kong, and by the time the war was over, they had earned seventeen decorations for bravery. In death, they were more than equal: more than 200 Native soldiers lost their lives on foreign battlefields during World War II.[4]

Native recruits joined up for many of the same reasons as their non-Native counterparts. Having lived through the Depression on reserves in mainly rural areas, they were eager to put behind the economic hardship of the past decade and to have jobs that provided some security. Patriotism, ideology, concern over spreading Nazism, and the example of their forefathers who served in World War I were other motivating factors.[5]

It has been suggested by some that the traditional Indian emphasis on "warriors" may have encouraged Natives to enlist as a means of achieving that status and prestige. With a reputation for being fearless and close to nature, the men were good hunters who were excellent scouts and snipers, and they excelled in any role that required climbing great heights. Fred Gaffen, author of *Forgotten Soldiers*, writes about the "warrior" prestige:

> Much more than in the white community, the warrior had prestige and status in traditional Indian society. For some Indians, the motive for enlisting was the opportunity to assert their manhood...
>
> In reading some accounts that earned Native Canadians military decorations on the battlefields of both World Wars, it becomes apparent that the skills of the Indian hunter and warrior came to the fore.[6]

Although their skills may have been appreciated on the battle-field, when Native soldiers returned to Canada, they were offered few of the benefits, such as education and training, given to their non-Native comrades whom they had served beside during World War II. The irony of their discriminatory treatment at the hands of the Canadian government in the postwar years was not lost on these ser-vicemen and women. It took nearly sixty years for Native veterans to receive the recognition and compensation they so deserved but for many, it was too late.[7]

Their war children too, have waited upwards of sixty years to find their fathers, and for many of these men and women — now in their late fifties and early sixties — it was also too late. In the following stories we hear how two war children, one Dutch and the other British, traced their roots back to Indian reservations in Canada. After they were reunited with their Canadian families, there were close relationships and they were accepted into the fold with much love and happiness.

NOTES

1. Also known as First Nations, Indian, Status Indian, Inuit, Metis, Native, Aboriginal and Aboriginal Canadians.

2. *Courage Remembered*, Canada's Digital Collections, Government of Canada. <http://collections.ic.gc/courage/nativeveterans.html>

3. Janice Summersby, *Native Soldiers, Foreign Battlefields* (Ottawa: Veterans Affairs, 1993), p. 20.

4. Summersby, p. 31.

5. Summersby, p. 21.

6. Fred Gaffen, *Forgotten Soldiers* (Penticton, B.C.: Theytus Books, 1985), p. 15. A recent announcement in the Fredericton *Daily Gleaner* (August 24, 2003, p. B4), illustrates the warrior prestige among Native soldiers. "Congratulations to PFC Young from family

and friends on her graduation from Basic Training.... Young is from the Kingsclear First Nation, N.B....Way to go... You are our Warrior."

7. *A Search For Equality* — National Roundtable Report, <http://ourworld.compuserve.com/homepages/aboriginal/rndtable.htm>. The 2001 report provides countless examples of systemic discrimination and humiliations against Native veterans, from being denied access to Canadian Legions because the Indian Act prevented them from entering establishments that sold alcohol, to being prevented from laying wreaths at local cenotaphs at Remembrance Day ceremonies. Not being allowed to enter Legions isolated Natives from sharing information with their comrades, who would have told them about the benefits to which they were entitled — a job that was supposed to be carried out by the Indian Agent on the Reserve who would not, or could not, advise veterans of their entitlements.

The Report of the Royal Commission on Aboriginal Peoples, 1996 <http://www.ainc-inac-g.ca/ch/rcap/sg/sgmm_e.html>, provides an in-depth examination of the historical relationship between Canada and its Native peoples. Volume 1, Part Two, Chapter 12.4 explores the experiences of Canada's Native veterans during and after World War II.

A Status Indian Living in Holland
by Olga Rains

Between the Dutch windmills and tulip fields stands a high totem pole. It belongs to Willy Van Ee, a member of the Sagamok Anishnawbek band of northern Ontario.

Willy is a war child, born in 1946 to a young Dutch woman and a Canadian status Indian. His father was a Canadian soldier who was stationed in the town of Utrecht. Willy's mother and father met after the liberation of Holland, and like thousands of other young Dutch women, she went out with the Canadian soldiers stationed in towns and cities throughout Holland.

Lloyd and Olga Rains and Willy Van Ee in a photo taken in front of the totem pole he erected in his front yard.

Soon, she became pregnant, and when Willy's father was repatriated to Canada, the relationship ended. She never heard from him again.

Willy's mother was luckier than other women who found themselves pregnant and alone when the Canadians left Holland. She married a Dutchman and had seven more sons and a daughter. Willy's stepfather was a good man who raised their oldest boy as though he were his own. In fact, Willy never knew that his father was a Canadian soldier, although he often wondered why he looked so different from his fairhaired siblings. With his dark hair, dark skin and almost Asiatic features, Willy certainly stood out next to the other members of his family, but it was never an issue, and Willy never asked.

The story of Willy's search for his father began in the 1960s, when he decided to emigrate to South Africa. Colonial ties made South Africa a popular destination for young Dutch men and women, despite its racist apartheid policy. Willy began the process of emigration, but when he went to the South African Embassy, they took one look at him and could see that he was not a racially "pure" white person. They asked for his birth certificate and in so doing, they opened up a Pandora's box that changed Willy's life forever.

On the birth certificate, the space for his father's name was blank. He asked his mother who his father was. She gave him a name, but it was not the right one. She also gave him a photograph of herself and Willy's father in uniform. Looking back at Willy were his mother and a good-looking young man then in his early twenties. The young couple looked happy and in love. It was quite a shock for Willy.

At that time, I was in Holland, appearing on a TV show about adoptees. After the show, Willy contacted us, and when we finally met him, the first thing he said was, "What nationality is my father? Is he Japanese or Italian or what?" He still had no idea his father was an Aboriginal Canadian.

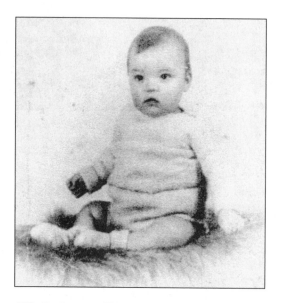

Willy Van Ee as a toddler. He often wondered if his father was Italian or Japanese. It never crossed his mind that he had Native Canadian roots.

We started searching for Willy's father, but we did not realize that we had the wrong name. With Willy's permission, we wrote a story and submitted it, along with the wartime photo of his mother and father, to numerous Canadian newspapers. One of Willy's relatives on Manitoulin Island read the article and wrote to us with information about Willy's father, whose name was Walter Mejaki.

Walter was a status Indian from the Sagamok Anishnawbek band on Manitoulin Island, in northern Ontario. He died in 1972, leaving behind an American wife whom he married shortly after returning from Europe. They had two sons, Willy's half-brothers, who live in the United States. According to the relative, Walter wanted to marry Willy's mother after the war, but the grandmother interfered and wouldn't let her son marry a European girl.

"They're no good," she said, and that was the end of Walter's wartime love affair. Like so many other Canadian soldiers in the same predicament, Walter never contacted his Dutch girlfriend and baby. Life went on.

The following summer, Willy and his wife visited the island and met many members of his father's family, who immediately welcomed him into the fold. Willy's visit to his father's ancestral homeland stirred a spiritual connection to the past and, when he returned to Utrecht, he built himself a totem pole as a measure of pride in his own Native heritage.

His father's American wife and family were not so forthcoming. Once Walter's identity was confirmed, Willy wrote to his widow in Milwaukee, Wisconsin, where she lived with Willy's two half-brothers. He was told in no uncertain terms by their lawyer to leave the Mejaki family alone.

> They have requested that I contact you with respect to your correspondence. Please be advised that during the lifetime of Mr. Mejaki, he never conveyed to them any knowledge of your existence or situation.... They have requested that you please do not contact them in the future in any manner whatsover. They merely want to be left alone.

It was a huge disappointment for Willy, but he didn't give up. It took many years and considerable red tape, but in 1986 he was finally confirmed by Canada's Department of Indian and Northern Affairs as a registered status Indian. Today, he holds the distinction of being the only Dutch-born citizen who is also a registered Aboriginal Canadian.

> "I am pleased to confirm that you are now registered as an Indian in the Indian Register in accordance withe provisions of paragraph 6(1) (a) of the Indian Act under the name of Wilhemus van Ee, born April 8, 1946."

Willy frequently visits his relatives in northern Ontario and has forged a solid relationship with them. On each trip "home," he learns more about his Aboriginal ancestry, their customs and traditions. And when his two sons turn eighteen, they will also become status Indians, bringing another generation into a cycle that began with a wartime love affair between a Dutch woman and a Canadian soldier from the Sagamok Anishnawbek band.

The Impact Has Been Enormous
by Melynda Jarratt

Josephine Gee was born in a home for unwed mothers at Brockett Hall, England, on May 20, 1945. Her mother, Lillian Miller, never married and raised Josephine alone with the help of her own parents.

When Josephine was nine years old, she found out that her father, Donald Potts, was a Native-Canadian soldier. This explained her dark complexion, which set her apart from other British children with their fair hair and light skin. Josephine remembers with fondness that her mother used to call her "my little papoose," a term of endearment that grew to have more significance as Josephine grew up.

Josephine learned that her father and mother dated for about six months. As the story goes, the last time Donald and Lillian saw each other, the baby was in a pram and he pressed a ten-pound note into her tiny hand.

Lillian died in 1993, and six years later Josephine contacted Project Roots for help in finding Donald Potts. The chances of finding him alive were remote: he had been thirty-seven years old when Josephine was born, and that would make him ninety-one by the time Project Roots began to look for him in Canada. We contacted several newspapers, and one, the North Bay *Nugget* in October 1999, led to her father's family in Temagami, a reserve on the Quebec-Ontario border.

Since then, Josephine has travelled to Canada and met her Canadian half-brothers, Roger and David Potts. Within a year of their first meeting, Roger passed away following a long struggle with cancer. In e-mails to Lloyd and Olga Rains before Roger died, he spoke happily about the reunion with his new-found sister and the joy she had brought into his life.

Canadian soldier Donald Potts, in a wartime photo. Potts was thirty-seven years old when Josephine was born. He was from Temagami, on the Quebec-Ontario border.

Josephine, too, was overwhelmed by the reception she received from her Canadian family and says the impact on her life "has been enormous." In this letter, dated May 2000, Josephine wrote to Olga and Lloyd.

Dear Olga and Lloyd:

I don't really know where to begin writing my story. Because the impact you have made on my life is so enormous. I feel that I owe you so much!

The photos I am sending you will show you that I am a part of this Canadian family. When we finally met, we found so many uncanny likenesses between both families that it took our breath away. For a start, Roger and David, my two half-brothers and I, all have our grandmother's eyebrows. We are all so alike in so many ways that it is like looking in the mirror. When I met Roger at the Toronto Airport, we didn't have to be introduced. It was the same with David in Ottawa.

Perhaps the most uncanny likeness is between my 22-year-old son Daniel and the 21-year-old son of my cousin Lorraine, who lives up in the Indian reservation, just inside the Quebec border. Roger and I were busy talking to my Aunt Gloria and some cousins, when suddenly, in walked Daniel's double, Rodney! He is the image of my son Daniel, same attractive smile, same everything!

I also visited my 85-year-old Aunt Annie who is in a Native-Canadian old people's home, and saw for myself how I will probably look in 30 years time.

Then I met my nephew Jeff. He is the image of how I used to look when I was younger. It is so strange and so wonderful to make all these discoveries.

And no, there is no Alzheimers in the family and no degenerative diseases, to my intense relief. There is alcoholism and obesity, although both missed my father, but no genetic time bombs are lying in wait for me.

I realize now more than ever how important it is to know one's roots and my heart goes out to the thousands of war children who do not know their Canadian fathers and families.

One of my dearest wishes was to see the places that my father knew and loved and grew up in. Evidently, he had many opportunities in life, including American high school education, but he was always drawn back to Temagami, north of North Bay, Ontario. It was there that he earned his living as a ferryman. But he had a heart condition and had to retire in his mid-fifties, when David practically took over the ferry business.

But is life not strange for I have ended up marrying a ferryman! My husband Michael is First Officer on one of the huge channel ferries.

You can imagine how I felt when I looked over Lake Temagami. By writing a poem I tried to describe my feelings.

I had always felt bitter that my mother never had any financial help from Canada while I was a child. But now I know that there was nothing available. David and Roger had an extremely hard upbringing and I was brought up in the lap of luxury compared to them.

Thank you once again for all you have done for us.

Josephine Gee's mother used to call her "my little papoose."

He Was Ecstatic
by Joan Kramer-Potts

Note: Joan Kramer-Potts was married to Roger Potts, the brother of Josephine Gee. Roger died soon after meeting his English sister. In this letter, Joan recalls their reunion in Canada and how important it was to Roger.

When Roger told me about having been contacted by Josephine, he was ecstatic. He has two brothers: one in Ottawa that he seldom saw and the other, a half-brother he hadn't seen for many years. He lost both his parents when he was in his early twenties.

Even though he was in his late forties when Josephine contacted him through Project Roots, the discovery of a sibling was just about the best thing that could have possibly happened to him at that time in his life. It was a chance to connect with a whole new family, a family that he could embrace.

His brother, David, and David's wife, Sandy, had two wonderful children whom he loved dearly, his nephew Jeff and niece Darcey. And now he had Josephine's children added to the equation. Roger was a happy man.

Josephine arrived at the Toronto airport and they recognized each other immediately. They had the same eyebrows, the same broad smile, those mischievous eyes that twinkle back at you. They had a lot of private time together, getting to know each other. Roger took Josephine to his favourite places: to Niagara Falls, New York, and to Pete's Marketplace, where they enjoyed dinner to the sound of his favourite honky-tonk piano player. He took her to Temagami, an Indian reserve on the Quebec-Ontario border, and introduced her to his Aunt Annie and his cousins.

They told her all about her father, the difficult life he had as a child, his success in the boxing ring. She learned about the Native-Canadian culture, the difficulties they all faced over the years. I believe Josephine found what had been missing in her life.

It is so unfortunate that Roger became ill shortly after their reunion. He was unable to attend Josephine's daughter's wedding, and as his health deteriorated, so did his will to connect. But I believe they came together at a time when each of them needed something wonderful to help them through difficult times. They laughed and played together like children. They shared their hopes and fears lovingly with each other just like brothers and sisters should.

Keep up the good work, Olga. I am sure there are a lot of happy endings out there just waiting to be found.

Josephine and her brother, Roger Potts, at their reunion in 2001.

Here are some excerpts from the e-mails Lloyd and Olga Rains received from Roger Potts during his visit with Josephine.

> Big sister is coming over on Wednesday, she is staying with me and is also going to Ottawa to visit David, her other brother....
>
> It's amazing knowing that I have a sister. I still have to pinch myself once in a while. It feels wonderful....
>
> Josephine and I are having the time of our lives. My sister is an absolute sweetheart and we are trying to catch up on some 50 odd years into weeks so you can imagine. We are going North this weekend to visit a couple of aunts and other relatives....
>
> My sister is a real Potts. We have so many similarities, it's amazing. Josephine and I even look alike. Our father sure left his mark. It feels like I have had a sister all my life which I have but just didn't know it. It feels great.

Mungwash
by Josephine Gee

The silken cord of memory reveals an ancient picture
A vivid, vibrant image, as yet unspoiled by time
Secrets that are passed down, in the hidden depths of memory
No, our ancestry can never be denied.
The picture's framed by pine trees, geese in V-formation
A strange and savage beauty, as yet unspoiled by man
Wide, white skys and silken lakes, stretching ever further
Yes, all of this is our ancestral land.
The sunlit ripples of the lake herald an intruder
As silently and swiftly, glides past a birch canoe
At one end sits a figure, paddling oh so lightly
His youthful, carefree moments, far too few.
Mungwash, son of lakes and forest
Son of nature's silver skies
Son of summer's lakeside lover
First born of his youthful mother
A child of the Ojibway tribe.
By the reeds, he ceased to paddle
Where soft breezes swayed the trees
His line, now carefully baited
While the forest watched and waited
For the advantage to be seized.
Dinner had been good that evening
The fish enough for all
Through the distant mist of years
Through so many hopes and fears
That night be still recalled.
The lake had never left his soul
It had always called him back
With him on the D-Day beach
Always there, just out of reach
In dreams, he trod the well-known tracks.
The brown hand on the ferry-wheel
Quickly wiped away a tear
Mungwash, had been welcomed home
He'd come back, he'd always known
To where his heart beat loud and clear.

Now, I see before me, as I stand upon that lakeside
The ugly scars and structures of uncaring modern times
Vandalizing, brutalizing — out of touch with nature
Killing so much natural beauty, sawing down the pine.
I, Mungwash's daughter, seeing for the first time
The shadow of my father's soul on Lake Temagami
Coming all the way from London, the city I grew up in
How much of this lies in my soul, too, and is part of me.

Children of Canadian Servicewomen
by Melynda Jarratt

"We gave them a cover story."

Canadian servicewomen at a dance with their male counterparts in England. Events like these often led to romance and romance led to sex and babies. A pregnant servicewoman could expect no mercy from her superiors.

Nearly 50,000 women enlisted in the Canadian armed services during World War II, but only one in nine, or about 1,000, served outside of Canada.[1] Although none of them ever held a combat role, they faced many of the same dangers as their male counterparts, including deadly German bombing raids. And like other young women in the U.K. and Europe during the war, some unmarried servicewomen became pregnant by Canadian soldiers and had their babies overseas.[2]

We don't know how many Canadians gave birth to illegitimate children, but we do know there were enough to warrant the assignment of a social worker to the Women's Division (WD) of the Royal Canadian Air Force, whose job it was to take care of pregnant WDs. Afraid of a scandal back home, the authorities gave the women a cover story and allowed them to have their babies in England. The babies were adopted, the servicewomen dismissed and sent home to resume their lives as though the pregnancy didn't happen.

Dismissal in Canada was one thing, but getting kicked out of the military in England because you were pregnant and unmarried was a scandal. One can imagine the web of lies a woman would have to spin to keep that story a secret and then to cover it up for a lifetime.

Canadian historian Ruth Roach Pierson, in her study of Canadian women during World War II, *They're Still Women After All*,[3] describes the problems unmarried pregnant servicewomen presented to military authorities during World War II. Pierson cites an opinion survey that was undertaken by the Canadian government in 1943, at the height of a whispering campaign that was working against female recruitment in the army and the air force.

The report was titled *An Enquiry into the Attitude of the Canadian Civilian Public towards the Women's Armed Forces*, and its results were distressing. According to the survey, there was a pervasive belief that women in the forces were promiscuous, immoral and loose, that some were former prostitutes, and that women joined the services to gain easy access to men — even married men. Among male family members, there was a very real fear that otherwise chaste sisters and daughters would become pregnant or contract venereal disease by joining the services.

These attitudes were difficult to break. Like most rumours and gossip about women and sex, they were rooted in the double standard about men and women's sexual behaviour and supported in part by the evidence of unmarried servicewomen who did contract VD or become pregnant while serving their country. For example, between December 1943 and December 1944, the incidence of pregnancy among unmarried members of the CWACS was 32.01 per thousand in Canada and 14.7 overseas. By comparison, the rate for the civilian population in 1941 was 10.4 per thousand.[4]

As noted by Jack Granatstein and Desmond Morton in their book *A Nation Forged in Fire*, the double standard was "very strong" and there were wild rumours about "troopships returning from England to North America full of pregnant CWACS."[5] Men, on the other hand, needn't worry: even though VD was far more commonplace among Canadian servicemen — and nearly 90 per cent of the fathers named by CWACs discharged for pregnancy were Canadians"[6] — men were generally unaffected by the troubles they caused for Canadian servicewomen. As Ruth Roach Pierson says in the chapter titled "Ladies or Loose Women?":

> It was almost expected of men in the forces to have a fling; any consequent "illegitimate" pregnancies were unfortunate, but primarily the women's responsibility;… men did not risk acquiring a bad reputation by joining the armed forces.[7]

In these short stories we will meet Chris, whose Canadian mother gave him up for adoption in England. We'll also meet Nano McConnell, a World War II veteran of the Women's Division who worked with pregnant Canadian servicewoman in England. Her observations of the human drama that unfolded during those years gives a different perspective on the war child story.

NOTES

1. "(W)ith the exception of the nursing sisters…", one in nine, or about 1,000 served outside of Canada. Alison Prentice et al. *Canadian Women: A History* (Toronto: Harcourt Brace Jovanovich, 1988), p. 302.

Also, in *Equal to the Challenge: An Anthology of Women's Experiences During World War II*, produced by Lisa Banister (Canada: The Department of National Defense, 2001), p. x. Canadian women were motivated to serve their country for many of the same reasons as men, and by the end of the war 21,624 had joined the Canadian Women's Army Corps (CWACS); 17,018 served in the RCAF Women's Division (WDs); and 6,781 signed up with the Women's Royal Canadian Naval Service (WRENS). In addition to the CWACS, WDs and WRENS, 4,581 served as nursing sisters in the Royal Canadian Army Medical Corps (RCAMC) and the medical branches of the RCN and RCA.

Also, in Jack Granatstein and Desmond Morton, *A Nation Forged in Fire* (Toronto: Lester & Orpen Dennys, 1989), p. 36.

2. Further research is required to determine the numbers of Canadian servicewomen who became pregnant by fellow Canadians and had illegitimate children overseas.

3. Ruth Roach Pierson, in Chapter 5, "Ladies or Loose Women?" of *They're Still Women After All: The Second World War and Canadian Womanhood*, (Toronto: McClelland and Stewart, 1986), pp. 169–87.

4. Further to this, Pierson notes that a study called "Special Report on Discharged Personnel June 1943" placed the blame for 86.3 per cent of the illegitimate pregnancies among CWAC personnel on Canadian servicemen. Pierson, *They're Still Women After All*, p. 172.

5. Granatstein and Morton, *A Nation Forged in Fire*, p. 36–37.

6. Prentice et al., *Canadian Women: A History*, pp. 302–03.

7. Pierson, *They're Still Women After All*, p. 173.

Thelma Left Her Baby in England
by Olga Rains

Chris was born in England in 1943 in a home for unwed mothers. He was adopted by an elderly couple and had a good but strict upbringing. Chris loved his mother and father, but being an only child with elderly parents was a problem. He was not allowed to climb trees or run in the yard. He felt like a sissy and wanted to rebel, but he never did.

As Chris grew older, he felt that something wasn't right in his life, but he couldn't put his finger on it. Chris boarded at private high school and only went home on holidays. His mother and father never came to see him, as their health was failing. Just before Chris went to university, his mom passed away and his dad went into a seniors' home.

The task of disposing of his parents' home and possessions was left to Chris. One day, while sorting through some documents, he found his adoption papers, complete with the names of his biological parents. To his complete surprise, he learned that both his parents were Canadians who had been stationed in England during World War II.

Chris took the papers and went over to his father's nursing home. His hands shaking, he showed his dad what he had found. The old man turned white and said nothing.

"Why wasn't I told?" Chris shouted at him. The old man started crying and told him that he had promised his wife never to tell Chris.

All Chris had were names. There were no place names in Canada or any other information. He tried his best to find out more, but every door he knocked on in England and Canada was closed to him.

As the years went by, Chris studied medicine and became a doctor. He met the girl of his dreams, married and became the father of twin boys. His life was busy, but never too busy to think of his biological parents, and whenever he had a chance he would try to find out more about them.

Years later, Chris picked up a newspaper, where he read a story about Project Roots. He contacted us, and we took what little information he had and started searching. The name of Chris's biological mother was unusual, but it was in many phone books throughout Canada, so it took a while to trace her.

After many phone calls, we found a family member who pointed us towards a very small village in Saskatchewan. Our letter to Thelma, Chris's mother, was not answered, and the follow-up phone call was greeted with sobs and screams.

A year later we were invited to a war bride reunion in Saskatoon, Saskatchewan. The village Thelma lived in was not too far from Saskatoon, so we decided to call her and arrange a short meeting. She begged us not to come, but we were determined to have a talk with her and show her a photo of Chris. After all, Chris also had a right to know more about his biological parents.

Thelma made sure we knew she was not one bit interested and that no one in her family knew about her English baby — nor would they ever know. The plan was for us to pick her up in the village — in front of the post office — and take her back to a restaurant in Saskatoon. She said she was scared because everyone in the village knew her.

The village had a few new houses, but most were dilapidated. There were no trees. There was a post office, a liquor store, two restaurants and a beer parlour. We sensed the village had a gossipy atmosphere and understood how Thelma would be wary of being seen in the company of strangers.

About one thousand Canadian women served overseas with the military during World War II. In this photo, the Canadian Inter-Servicewomen's Sports and Social Committee meet to discuss their plans.

Thelma was a sickly person who looked much older than she really was. She told us right away about all of her and her husband's illnesses and all the medication they took every day. We heard a long story about the problems her children had had — alcoholism and divorce.

When we showed her Chris's photo, she turned her head away and did not want to look or to hear anything about him. Next, we asked her about Chris's father. At first, she was tight-lipped. We had to promise not to search for him or else she would not reveal his name. Thelma told us that he was ten years older than her and that he had been a flight captain in the Royal Canadian Air Force. They had known each other for about a year and when she became pregnant, he just left her. He was a married man and had a wife and child in Canada.

Later, we did search for Chris's father and found out he had passed away six years earlier.

After explaining the whole situation to Chris, he was disappointed, but he appreciated all we had done for him. Being a very understanding person, he felt it was best to leave his biological mother alone. We did give Chris her address, but we are certain he will never use it.

This English son is just one of thousands who has experienced this kind of heartbreak.

Double Standard
by Nano Pennefeather-McConnell

Note: Nano McConnell was a member of the Women's Division of the Royal Canadian Air Force who served in London, England, during the war. Nano was responsible for helping pregnant servicewomen deal with the administrative, social and emotional issues that arose from their out-of-wedlock pregnancy. She helped them through the birth and thereafter, with the baby's adoption and the mother's repatriation to Canada.

My job in the Women's Division at RCAF Headquarters in London, England, was to meet new needs as they arose, so our job descriptions expanded to answer them. Many of the practical day-to-day needs we were called upon to fill were far from anything I had been prepared for in basic training. They could range from visiting the babies in a nursery or foster home, to arranging for extra orange juice rations at the Town Hall, to buying a laundry basket to make into a crib.

Canadian servicewomen who became pregnant — married or unmarried — were sent home. If they reported their condition too late to make the ocean crossing, they had their babies in England and were then repatriated. That was policy … until Lilith.

It's not surprising that so many young women became pregnant in those days. Selling or advertising birth control was illegal. Sex education did not exist. Society treated women who bore children outside marriage with contempt. Most families hid their unwed pregnant daughters so that their secret would be known to as few people as possible.

Nano Pennefeather-McConnell in her Women's Division (WD) uniform, 1942.

A few of the Canadian servicewomen I worked with had support from their families and kept their babies. Some who were desperate went through the very dangerous procedure of an out-of-hospital illegal abortion, risking their health, their lives and their freedom. Men might be trained to fight and kill, but women were charged with a criminal offence if they had an abortion.

Even today, when veterans get together, topics such as "illegitimate" babies or fear in the line of duty are rarely talked about. Discipline and following orders are supposed to take care of unacceptable feelings. If you don't follow the rules, you have to accept the consequences: man or woman, you're alone.

But in those days, the men got away with a lot more than the women. There was a double standard in the military that most people would find old-fashioned, ridiculous and illegal today. On the one hand, servicewomen were advised to wait for marriage before having sex, but servicemen were given information and condoms to prevent venereal disease.

There was a sympathetic attitude towards predatory men who had sex irresponsibly. They were often moved to another area while things cooled down, but if the woman was unlucky enough to get pregnant, it was all her fault and she was drummed out of the service. And since men denied paternity, there was very little these servicewomen could do to stake a claim for child support.

Perhaps I am judging the men too harshly: some might have taken responsibility had they known before they were killed that they had fathered a child. But the numbers of Canadian servicewomen who were left with children from men who were alive and well at war's end speak for themselves.

My work was unsettling, and depressing at times. It was also very challenging. It gave me an opportunity to learn more about human behaviour, but it left me with many unanswered questions. As the situations were confidential, I couldn't really talk to many people outside the office. With the publicity given to the lost files in the Somalia affair, I was reminded how I handled the women's confidential files.

The normal procedure was to requisition files from Central Registry and then return them with whatever action we had taken. I knew that even though the files were marked "Confidential," many people had access to them, and I was concerned about protecting their privacy.

As I remember, I quite often kept letters or other details relating to women and their babies in a file in the Women's section. Then, when that airwoman was posted away or back to Canada, I would return the missing material to the regular file. Of course, this was against regulations but we were making up our own rules about our own files in a lot of unprecedented situations.

While I want this story to be told, my original commitment to confidentiality means that I did not keep any record, nor do I have any memory of the real names of these women. I also don't have the names of the putative fathers of their children — if these were ever recorded. Therefore, these stories are composites, drawn from my memory of people and events that occurred a long time ago.

* * *

A strange scene was taking place outside the commanding officer's door at Overseas Headquarters. Three WDs were preparing to line up to march in. Two wore hats and sergeant's stripes; the one in the middle left her hat on a desk and was giggling as she tried to button her tight tunic over her expanding waist. I had a hard time to keep from laughing myself at the ludicrous scene.

Missing an overseas draft in wartime was called "desertion" and was serious enough to warrant a court-martial. Lilith had been posted back to Canada and was told to report to the embarkation port in Scotland at a certain date. Pregnant but not married, she was determined to stay in England to have her baby. She was waiting to tell the sailor/father about the baby when he came back to port. She went absent without leave until she was certain that her troopship would have sailed. She then reported to headquarters.

The CO had to remand the case that morning while he conferred with the judge advocate general's office (JAG) on how to handle this precedent-setting situation. Meanwhilem Lilith was ordered confined to barracks under guard. Since we had no barracks, she was remanded to the custody of three women sergeants — us. We all had to sleep at one of the apartments and return to headquarters in the morning with our "prisoner."

Lilith made light of the whole situation. She would leave the door open when she went to the bathroom so that she wouldn't be out of our sight.

The JAG and the commanding officer finally concluded that there was no punishment available for her "crime." It was now too late in her pregnancy to travel to Canada under wartime conditions. Lilith was given leave until her baby was born. She asked to stay at our apartment until she found her own accommodation. Lilith's sailor friend was sympathetic, but unable to take any responsibility for his child because he was already married with a family.

Lilith asked to be referred to an adoption agency as she saw no way of keeping the baby on her own. While little Cora was waiting to be adopted through the National Adoption Society in London, we placed her in a nursery that had been recommended by them.

One weekend, my flatmate and I went to visit Cora and were upset and saddened by the minimal physical care the overworked nurses were able to give. There was no time for holding or cuddling. We had on file an offer to care for children from a Canadian woman living in London. After consulting with the officer in charge of the section, I brought Cora to this new home.

There she was given loving care until her adoption. Lilith wrote from her station:

> Things are going pretty well at work. I have a bad cold and get pretty tired as the work is rather strenuous, but will get hardened in time and will be okay. Glad you got the papers, etc. all okay and that Cora is fine. I'm happy you moved her. Thank you for paying the board bill. I am enclosing it with the three pounds for the foster mother. Hope it won't be too much trouble for you. I can send it to her directly if you like. Just let me know. You have done so much for me already and it is sincerely and deeply appreciated, but I don't want to impose on you.

One aspect of my job was to escort the woman and her baby to the point of embarkation. Because we had no barracks in London, the easiest plan for all concerned was to have the mother and child come to my apartment after discharge from the hospital. Later, we were able to use the facilities of the Canadian Army Convalescent Hospital for women in Alderbroke.

Once she had settled in with the baby, Lilith wrote me from Canada:

> I had a very nice trip back. The baby was very good, he wasn't any trouble at all. I waited in Ottawa two weeks for my discharge, from there I went to the town where I enlisted and the Children's Aid had a home for my baby in less that two weeks. You have no idea how much I miss him, even yet. I guess I always will. My family doesn't know anything

about why I got my discharge. I do hope you girls over there don't get hit with a rocket plane, they seem to be taking a lot of lives.

* * *

I had to take a train once to visit a farm home where Iris was staying with her baby while awaiting adoption. She had really thought the baby's father intended to marry her. In those days we didn't talk about the fine line between mutual consent and submission. This shy young woman had been swept off her feet by empty promises. Now she was left alone with a child she would have to give up.

* * *

Judy and Tom were very much in love. He was a pilot with Bomber Command and whenever he came to London he stayed at her apartment. She often spent weekends in the town near his station. One morning I met her in the hall. She asked me to have lunch with her as she had some big news to tell me.

Since I was on duty in our section that noon hour, I suggested she bring me a sandwich from the canteen. As I waited for her, I started to read the latest edition of *Wings Abroad*. An item leaped out at me about raids over Berlin. Tom was reported "Missing Believed Killed."

Just then, Judy bounced in, handed me my sandwich with one hand and held out the other to show me her diamond-and-emerald engagement ring: "Tom and I are getting married next month!"

I didn't know what to say.

She went on. "What's the matter? I thought you would be happy that we were finally going to make it legal."

Slowly I turned the paper around and pointed to Tom's name. I held her as she sobbed her heart out.

A few weeks later, Judy realized she was pregnant. She was determined to keep her baby. We made enquiries with the legal department. She discovered she could legally change her name to be the same as Tom's before her baby was born.

All this seems so unnecessary today, when the term "illegitimate child" is no longer used. But in those days, the double standard towards men and women and the taboo against unwed pregnancy made "illegitimacy" a very real concern. An unmarried woman with child had to face lasting consequences that no one could predict.

186

Child of War
by Nano Pennefather-McConnell

Gliding over new fallen snow
past a country graveyard
I come upon an orchard
where apple seedlings swaddled in white tape
stretch across the field and become
white crosses in a military cemetery
my eyes deceived by time
see three figures in Air Force blue
walking between the crosses
the chaplain cradles a small white coffin
in the crook of his arm
I walk silently beside another airwoman
wanting so much to comfort her
while she buries her baby
I know nothing of her story
only that she is alone
and I have been assigned to be with her
we pass a monument to the Unknown Soldier
did he die without knowing his child? —
"in green pastures he lets me lie down" —
the white coffin is laid in the grave
there are no marching airman
no muffled drums no bugles playing
"day is done"
this day in Aldershot
the mother walks slowly back over the frozen ground
her composure
forbids any offer of sympathy —
"it was good of you to come" —
the service is over
air force regulations leave no time for mourning
our transportation arrives
she returns to the hospital and I go back to London
there are no monuments to children
born of war
no white crosses
only surfacing memories
and these white-stemmed apple seedlings
in a Canadian orchard

Chapter 7

The Canadians in Occupied Germany
by Melynda Jarratt

"It was unbearable at times,
but together we came through it."

Life went along as usual under the occupying forces in Germany at the end of the war. In this photo, a group of young German women attend a party in Berlin hosted by Allied soldiers.

Much has been written about the early days following the war and tensions between defeated Germans and their Allied occupiers, but little has been said about the relations between Canadian soldiers and the women they met in occupied Germany.

What we find is a familiar pattern: in Germany, as in the United Kingdom, Holland and Belgium, young women who found themselves pregnant by Canadian soldiers could expect no mercy from their families and countrymen, nor from the Canadian authorities.

It is important to note that the German situation was different from that of Holland and Belgium, where liberating Canadians were greeted with joyous pandemonium and wild drinking binges went on for weeks at dances throughout the country. In Holland, the Canadians were welcomed, at least until the pregnancies started to show.

Germany was the enemy, and its occupiers could not expect the same reception they had been met with in Holland and Belgium. Sensitive to public sentiment back home in Canada and eager to restore social order in a country that had just been defeated, the question of how to deal with relations between the occupying soldiers and local German women was handled by an immediate and outright ban on fraternization.

Anti-fraternization regulations were widely distributed throughout the Canadian, U.S., British and other allied forces by the Supreme Headquarters, Allied Expeditionary Force (SHAEF), but within one month, SHAEF lost the battle.

Love has a way of circumventing regulations, and Canadian soldiers with lots of time on their hands were bound to have a social life that involved local women. There was little the Canadian military could do to prevent it.

Writing in June, 1945 the Military Government Bureau of SHAEF noted of the German situation:

> ... although it would be wrong to say that the non-fraternization order has broken down, it is abundantly clear that a few coaches-and-fours have already been driven through it..."[1]

That same month, prohibitions against speaking with children were loosened. In July, non-fraternization was amended to allow conversations with adults, and in September the policy was dropped entirely.[2]

When soldiers started going out with local women, the results were inevitable. The lucky ones got married, but as we saw elsewhere at the end of the war, thousands of single German women found themselves pregnant and unwed in an unforgiving society that was reeling from the shock of defeat.

Interestingly, in Germany, the anti-fraternization movement had some home-grown supporters: returning German veterans, battle-weary soldiers and idealistic Nazi youth who felt betrayed by their countrywomen openly courting the occupiers.

A study of U.S.–German relations by Perry Biddiscombe, which appeared in the *Journal of Social History* in June 2001, describes a violent anti-fraternization movement in Germany which led to the death of at least one U.S. soldier when he was attacked by a group of former veterans for daring to go out with a German woman.

But that was the extreme. In the main, the German veterans targeted women, attacked them when they were alone or with a foreign soldier, and brutally shaved their heads as a sign of disapproval. Other manifestations of the movement resulted in anonymous, threatening letters, anti-fraternization posters stuck on poles and the sides of buildings, and the painting of graffiti on the homes of suspected women.

In such a world, there was little consideration or sympathy for pregnant, single German women whose Canadian boyfriends had abandoned them. Like the U.S. example, where an estimated 30,000 children were born of U.S. soldiers and German women, the Canadian military adopted a policy of "taking no responsibility for illegitimate children fathered by occupation troops."

How many German-Canadian war babies were born is unknown, but as the paper trail that flows through Beverly's story shows, when her father decided he didn't want anything more to do with his German girlfriend and baby, the Canadian authorities helped him all the way. Less is known about Heiko Windels' story, and more may only come to light when his father is located — dead or alive. In any case, employing the same tactics that had worked so well throughout the war in the U.K., and later, after the Liberation of Holland and Belgium, Canada took no responsibility for the children fathered by its personnel stationed in Germany.

NOTES:

1. PRO FO 371/46933, SHAEF G-5 "Political Intellegence Letter" no 0, 4 June, 1945, as quoted in Perry Piddiscombe, "Dangerous Liaisons: The Anti-Fraternization Movement in the U.S Occupation Zones of Germany and Austria, 1945–1948, *Journal of Social History*, June 2001, pp. 611–47.

2. *The Stars and Stripes* (South Germany Edition), 14 June, 1945, as quoted in Piddiscombe.

3. "Pregnant Frauleins are Warned," *The Stars and Stripes*, 8 April, 1946, as quoted in Piddiscombe.

I Was Born in Germany
by Susanne Werth

Beverly-Susanne is my name. It was given to me by my father, Leslie William Barden, a Canadian soldier who met my mother, Maria Franzen, when he was a member of the Allied occupation force in Germany at the end of World War II.

My mother became pregnant, and they were engaged to be married, but before the ceremony took place my father was repatriated to Canada. Soon after, on December 18, 1946, I was born.

My father wrote letters to my mother every week, mainly about the expected child. I still have all of them, with all the names he suggested. My mother saved all his letters and passed them on to me and, in turn, I will pass them on to my children.

On November 18, 1946, a month before I was born, my mother received an official letter from the Department of Mines and Resources, Immigration Branch, in Canada. The commissioner told her that my father had made an application for her admission to Canada, and that all the settlement arrangements were satisfactory. It was noted that the expected child would be included.

At the same time, suddenly and without any reason, my father stopped writing. Then, on March 3, 1947, another official letter arrived from the Immigration Branch — and this time it was bad news. My father wished no further action and that our case be deferred as he was unable to assume any obligations at the present time. Therefore, settlement arrangements could no longer be considered satisfactory for us, and the department's approval for our admission to Canada was withdrawn. (See letters in the appendix, pages 215–217.)

Susanne's mother, Maria Franzen, fully expected to come to Canada with her baby, but her Canadian boyfriend changed his mind.

On May 21, 1947, another letter from the same department arrived, asking my mother to return the letter dated November 18, 1946, in which approval had been granted. I guess they wanted to make sure we stayed in Germany. What a heartless way to treat my poor mother! First she had to cope with the loss of my father, and then the Canadian government let her know that she wasn't welcome!

It was always my greatest wish to become acquainted with my father and the grandfather of my three children, but I didn't know how to go about doing it. My mother had told me from my earliest childhood about my father. Believe me when I say that life for my mother and me in Germany was very severe. Women who had children by soldiers from the occupying forces were ostracized and tormented. I am not exaggerating. It was unbearable at times, but together we came through it all.

I always wondered how my father and his family would accept me. Fifty-one years later, I found out. In 1997, I started the search with the help of Project Roots. He was found, and was very surprised that I was looking for him — he pretended not to know anything — so Project Roots wrote to him explaining everything along with photos of my mother and me. He did not answer that letter, so two weeks later they called him again, and a lady answered telling them that he wasn't home and that he had not received any letter.

So another letter was sent, and again no answer. Another phone call was made, and again he wouldn't come to the phone, but after they persisted, he finally did. He admitted that he was that soldier in the photo they sent him, but as it was fifty years later, he could not remember anything. When asked if they could give his address to me, he agreed. I wrote a long letter to him, but he never answered.

There was no doubt in my mind that he was deeply ashamed of himself for what he had done to my mother and me after the war, but I'll never know. He passed away on December 30, 1997, before I could get any answers to what happened in those days around my birth.

In the meantime, Project Roots had continued the search for my Canadian family and found an aunt and an uncle — a sister and a brother of my father. They were not all that happy in the beginning, either, and my letters to them were not answered for a long time — and not until after Project Roots had approached the younger generation of this family.

I tried to explain how important it was for me to know my Canadian roots. It took time, but I was patient and waited and gave these people lots of room. With every letter I sent this family, I had enclosed copies of some old letters my father had written, papers of the Immigration Branch and the envelope which had been sent back to my mother in 1949 with the word "Deceased" on it. Finally someone answered, and to my surprise she signed the letter "Auntie."

Leslie William Barden in a wartime photo. Leslie changed his mind and withdrew sponsorship of his German girlfriend and baby.

I was so happy. The ice was broken!

In 1998, my daughter Bettine and I planned a trip to Canada to meet my aunt and her family. During the preparations for this trip, visitors arrived at my door. What a surprise: there was Aunt Mary, her daughter and granddaughter. They were visiting friends on the Dutch-German border, and because their curiosity was greater than their former distance, they wanted to become acquainted with their new German addition to the family. Still, the atmosphere was very stiff and reserved. They avoided speaking about my father or about the years after the war. In my opinion, Aunt Mary is very intelligent, but inaccessible. She showed inability to accept the truth.

The next year, Bettina and I visited Canada, and the trip was very successful. We were welcomed and they made us feel like part of the family. My daughter and I felt very comfortable, and the conversations were pleasing. Unfortunately, they had had very little contact with my father in the past, so they didn't know very much about him. I did find out lots of information about my grandparents and my Canadian roots and I am very happy about that.

Like Winning a Lottery!
by Ron and Diane Matthews

It was quite a surprise for us to find out we had a cousin in Germany — one with a family and a whole life story to tell us. I'm sure you see many different reactions to finding a family for a war child: anger, fear, the cup half-empty worrying about the missed times, and then the cup half-full that thinks about what could and can be, now and into the future.

It is my belief that we have taken the latter view — let's not worry about or dwell on what was or what could have been, but on what can be. How lucky can you get? Finding new family and making new friends all at the same time — it was like winning a lottery!

We've already come a long way, getting together and doing things, and although we have discussed the past, we haven't dwelled on it — what's done is done, so let's move forward and enjoy each other as best we can, recognizing that we live many miles away.

But the miles haven't stopped us so far. Already we've shared numerous joyous hours sharing our daily lives — work, pastimes, hobbies, etc. — just doing and showing each other what we do on a daily basis; just getting to know each other. We've visited each other's homes and vacationed together, evenings at the pub after a day at work and had more fun than a bunch of school children. There have been trips to Canada and Germany and a birthday party (I couldn't make it — I know they understand) in New Orleans.

In a very short time we've shared much joy, and unfortunately much sorrow, with the death of my mother last April. We've also been able to get the next generation, our children, together — that was pretty special for all of us.

My son proudly wears his German soccer team sweater and colours and loved to order the *brötchen* (rolls) in Germany during our visit and still talks about it. He is also looking forward to the next World Cup so we can see it in Germany, as well as to seeing a Formula I race with Uncle Wolf and maybe taking another spin on the *Grüne Holle*. My daughter will always remember being taken to a doctor's office in East Germany and being cared for by me — but mostly Beverly — while her mother and brother ventured further into East Germany with Uncle Wolf.

They will also remember eating many different foods, including rabbit for the first time — something I would never have been able to talk them into.

Whether it was visiting the cathedral in Köln, or Grandma in Kleve, taking a walk to the pub or just enjoying each other's company over dinner, a whole new world has been opened up for all of us.

Not many people get this kind of opportunity. We talk to each other and write to each other regularly (a whole new dimension to life), we also gain their three children and spouses, whom we greatly enjoyed already, talking sports or finance, shopping and learning German and even getting some free medical advice — not a bad start. We've learned much already from our new family and have much more to learn and enjoy.

Surprisingly enough, we have much in common — love for family, joy and pride in our children, friends, music (a scary fondness for Leonard Cohen), Gummi Bears, auto racing and fast cars, German beer, grappa, castles, churches and nice wine, even faulty thyroids, just to name a few. You choose your friends and not your family, but in this case we lucked out because we couldn't have chosen any better.

Though we do need to come to grips with the past and we do sometimes just want and need to discuss the past, I think that there is also a recognition that we will never be able to really understand, nor can we change, what went on before, so let it be — concentrate on what you can influence and make the best of it. We're already making our own past and wonderful memories!

To date we've just scratched the surface of this wonderful new relationship and are looking forward to sharing more of the things I've mentioned above as well as things we haven't even imagined yet. This is just the beginning.

Susanne (second from left) with her newfound Canadian family. Susanne proves that a little bit of forgiveness and understanding can go a long way for the Canadian war children of World War II.

Who Knows Jim Thomson?
by Heiko Windels

I was born in Varel, Germany, on September 20, 1946. My unmarried German mother, Amanda, met my Canadian father, Jim Thomson, who was stationed in Varel, Germany. She lived at Bahnhofstrasse 45 in Varel.

I did not know until June 2001, that my father was a Canadian soldier by the name of Jim Thomson. I knew that I was an illegitimate child, but nobody ever told me about my father, what nationality he was or what happened to him after the war.

I never had the courage to confront my parents about my biological father. This was something no one talked about. My mother died in 1998 and she took her secret to the grave.

Heiko Windels found this photo of Jim Thomson among his late stepfather's possessions.

When my stepfather, Adolf Windels, died in June 2001, I found this photo of my Canadian father, Jim Thomson. I also found a letter, dated April 7, 1946, in which my father expresses his deep love for my mother and confirms my upcoming birth. If you know Jim Thomson, please contact Project Roots.

Postscript: On page three of the four-page letter, Jim Thomson wrote to Amanda about their coming baby and how sad he was that he could not be there.

> As a result of our passionate love a child will be born and I am jealous that I can't be there to share this happiness with you. My heart and soul will always be with you both.
>
> Jim

My Dad
by Margaret

Why are you always in my mind?
Why do I have to care?
There are so many years gone in my life
I've very much wished you could share.

I try to imagine how you looked then
In the year of '44
A young Canadian airman
Over here to fight a war

I wonder if you have thought of
The girl you left behind
Carrying your unborn child
Did you really mind ?

Have you tried to find me?
Like I have searched for you
It could be that you lost your life
I can't believe that's true

No one but us can understand
Why we alone must search
Through all the disappointments
The emptiness and hurt

It's really not important
If you are good or bad
Because nothing in the world, can take away
The fact that you are my dad

Perhaps you even need me
If you do I'm over here
Across the wide Atlantic
Our blood bond holds me near

I pray soon my search will be over
And we make contact at last
My self and my Canadian
My dad from out of my past.

Chapter 8

By Virtue of His Service
by Melynda Jarratt

"The uniform covers a lot."

Canadian veterans march in the parade to mark the fortieth anniversary of the Dutch Liberation, Apeldoorn, 1985. It was at a parade like this in 1980 that Lloyd and Olga Rains heard about the Dutch war children of World War II and Project Roots was born.

> "No provision is made for financial aid to mothers of illegitimate children or for the care and maintenance of such children." — Hon. D.C. Abbott, Minister of National Defence, December 9, 1946.[1]

"The uniform covers a lot" was a saying that made the rounds in Great Britain during World War II. It referred to young Allied servicemen —

Canadians, Americans, New Zealanders and Aussies — who may have looked good in uniform, but were earning a bad reputation for getting single — and even married — women into "trouble." Thousands of these young men met women in England and Europe during the war. Romances bloomed and love led to sex and babies.

An estimated 30,000 Canadian war children were born in Britain and Europe during World War II — some 22,000 in England alone, another six to seven thousand in Holland after that country was liberated.[2] Their mothers were mainly teenagers and young women, but there were older, married women as well, driven by loneliness after years of separation from husbands who were serving in the Mediterranean, North African and European theatres of war, or who were PoWs in Germany and Japan. In the absence of eligible men, the Canadians filled the gap, and the thousands of war children were the result.

Olga Rains (left) with four Dutch war children whom she has helped through Project Roots.

Although it would be a sweeping generalization to say all the Canadian servicemen who fathered children overseas had no conscience, many certainly fit the description. Some were single men just out for a good time, thirty years and older who didn't even see the fighting. They stayed in England doing desk jobs, so they had plenty of time on their hands. Others were married and had families in Canada. Some were bigamists. When they went back to Canada, they were never heard from again by their girlfriends and children.

To be fair, many fathers would gladly have taken on their responsibilities had they been given a chance. Some men were killed in action and never even knew their lovers were pregnant. Other servicemen were removed from the area by their commanding officers at the request of the woman's angry parents. Many families interfered in the courting, confiscating letters and basically destroying the relationships.

Still other men and women were legally married, but the fairy-tale wartime union did not survive real life in postwar Canada. In addition to the unknown number of war brides who came to Canada and then returned with their children over the years, an estimated 4,000 of the nearly 48,000 war brides never even came to Canada on the free transportation scheme. Reasons varied, but for many Canadian servicemen there were better opportunities in the U.K. and Europe, so the men took their discharge in Britain and raised their families overseas. But a significant number of women refused offers of free passage on the war bride ships due to "marital estrangement" or "unsatisfactory settlement arrangements."[3] The evidence is in the files of the Canadian Wives Bureau, where page after page lists the names of hundreds of women who refused to come to Canada because their wartime marriages did not work out. For this group, there were divorce and custody battles, unpaid child support and all the shame that went with the stigma of a failed marriage in the 1940s.

What makes the war child story even more tragic is evidence of a discriminatory wartime policy that denied assistance to unmarried women seeking help for themselves and their children, from child support to transportation to Canada under the fiancée category. As the military and civilian agencies responsible for the social problems of servicemen's dependents in the U.K. and Europe, the Department of National Defence, Veterans Affairs, and the Immigration Branch of Mines and Resources decided that public funds would be spent only on entitled servicemen's dependents — war brides who had legally married overseas.[4] Unwed mothers and their children did not qualify for assistance and were therefore denied any help whatsoever.

Such was the prejudice against unwed mothers that an unfounded rumour about unmarried Dutch women and their children coming to Canada ahead of other fiancées sparked the protest of a George

Gillespie, who wrote a letter of complaint to his member of Parliament, Ralph Maybank, in July 1947.

> These women and their babies have not only been given free passage but were given preference to the shipping arrangements to the decent engaged girls who sought to come to Canada to marry their fiancées.[5]

It was this kind of attitude that permeated the entire military and civilian bureaucracies and was manifested in its reaction to the "residual problems" of Canadian servicemen in postwar Britain. On November 7, 1946, the minister of Defence, having just returned from a visit to the U.K., asked the sub-committee of the cabinet for a government decision on four problems:

a) dependents remaining overseas, even those who may never come to Canada;

b) bigamous marriages;

c) unmarried mothers (paternity acknowledged by Canadian servicemen);

d) unmarried mothers (paternity not acknowledged by Canadian servicemen).

Over the course of the next thirty minutes, the sub-committee decided that items c) and d) were no longer going to be on the agenda, and with a stroke of a pen they cut off any further discussion of the issue. That's essentially the way things have stood since 1946.[6]

In a politically and socially charged environment where unwed mothers could expect no sympathy from the authorities, every agency with the power to help simply passed the buck to somebody else. Not surprisingly, it was the charitable organizations that ultimately had to deal with Canada's illegitimate children, a problem that became increasingly pronounced as servicemen began to leave the U.K. in 1945 and 1946.

As the men were repatriated, their former girlfriends and wives overwhelmed the Canadian Wives Bureaus in London and on the continent for assistance with legal aid and child support. The Bureau drew the line at unwed mothers, insisting it was responsible only for the transportation of legally married war brides who qualified for all manner of assistance as wives of Canadian soldiers. These services included dependent's allowance and free transportation to Canada. Services to married wives also included legal aid in cases of marital estrangement.

But as we have seen, in the cases of war brides who tried to get child support, that service was sorely lacking.[7]

Depending on whether the man was still enlisted, the problem went to DND or Veterans Affairs, who in turn passed it on to organizations like the Family Welfare Association.[8] But even though it was fully aware of the problems of unwed mothers, the Bureau, and its bosses in the government, simply refused to help unwed mothers. These agencies could get away with it because they knew full well there would be no public outcry on behalf of these social outcasts, and they were absolutely right.

At the end of 1946, with nearly 65,000 war brides and their children having arrived in Canada, the Wives Bureau closed up its offices overseas and handed over the responsibility of servicemen's dependents to Veterans Affairs and the Immigration Branch. In effect, the DND washed its hands of any further involvement with the social problems caused by the Canadians in the U.K. and Europe — including unwed mothers and their children. Unfortunately, so did the agencies it had entrusted with the same task.

As late as April 1947, the Canadian High Commissioner in England, N.A. Robertson, reported that no public funds were being spent on unwed mothers. Rather, these women and their children in the U.K. were being "referred to the social agency known as the National Society for the Unmarried Mother and Her Child," which drew upon monies raised by the Toronto *Evening Telegram* for the British War Victims Fund. In 1946 alone, the fund provided $15,000 to unwed mothers through the Canadian Overseas Children's Fund, which redistributed the money to needy families in the U.K. so as to avoid any perception that government authorities were involved.[9]

Adding to the problems of unwed mothers was the policy of the Departments of National Defence and Veterans Affairs to deny unwed mothers access to information about the whereabouts of soldiers still serving overseas or those who had been discharged in Canada. Many a letter was written in vain to Canadian officials, asking for help in tracing a veteran, but the responses and denials were always the same, expressing the usual regrets that the relevant branch or department could not provide the information requested, etc. In some cases, letters to a soldier's home address were returned with the words "deceased" on the envelope, suggesting the veteran had been killed in action or died of his injuries after returning to Canada, so as to discourage further inquiry.

Olga and Nellie den Teuling, a Dutch war child whose father was found with the help of Project Roots.

In an interview before he passed away in 2002, Colonel Blake Oulton of the North Shore Regiment of New Brunswick recalled an incident during the war when a pregnant English woman and her parents came to the North Shore's English base demanding to confront the responsible Canadian soldier. As was the practice, Colonel Oulton denied the request and effectively put an end to any further inquiry when he told the family, "It takes two to tango."[10]

As the symbols of male authority and power, the military played along with prevailing social attitudes towards women and sex, which planted the blame — and the shame — for an illegitimate baby on the mother alone. Historian Ruth Roach Pierson has explored the issue of the sexual double standard in her groundbreaking study of Canadian women during World War II called *They're Still Women After All.* Citing wartime polls, studies, correspondence and policy, she shows how women were either "ladies or loose women" in the eyes of society and the military establishment.[11] Such treatment of children and single mothers would not be tolerated today, but with the denial of information that still goes on in 2004, why is it deemed acceptable for Canada's war veterans?

In a practice that has continued uninterrupted since the end of World War II, access to information contained in the files at the National Archives in Ottawa remains closed to inquiring war children. This is true even for those children whose parents were married, as we have seen in the stories about war brides whose marriages ended in separation or divorce. If a Canadian veteran dies today, the Privacy Act ensures that it will be twenty years before his child can obtain identifying information in the military personnel records housed at the Archives. These files contain what may be the war child's only hope of finding his or her roots, but a veteran's records are protected like a military secret. Not one scrap of information — not even his military registration number — will be released to a war child.

The plight of the war children points to one of the many contradictions in the Canadian government's treatment of fathers and their children today. In 2005, if a Canadian man fathers a child, whether he is a serviceman or not, the government's legal services and child support regulations swing into action. Social attitudes and legislation are such that any father refusing to acknowledge his paternity or pay child support can be taken to court, forced to take a DNA test and have his wages garnisheed for upwards of eighteen years or until the child finishes university. But in the 1940s, it was considered a rite of passage for a young man to sow his wild oats before getting married, and it was acceptable to simply walk away when his girlfriend got pregnant. The girlfriend, on the other hand, could bear no greater shame than to be pregnant and unmarried with the child of a Canadian soldier. Ostracized by their families, stereotyped as loose women, and with no financial support from the fathers or governments in the pre–welfare state, is it any wonder so many gave their children up for adoption rather than take on the task of raising the child alone?

By today's standards, it's unlikely the Canadian military would tolerate such boorish behaviour. Family law and societal attitudes towards parental responsibility have changed. Today, we demonize men who walk out on their children by calling them "bums" and "deadbeats." When young servicemen get their girlfriends or wives pregnant today, they have a legal and ethical responsibility to support children financially when the relationship ends, but not veterans of World War II. Why?

By virtue of his service, the Canadian World War II veteran was rendered untouchable by a male military tradition that protected him sixty years ago and continues to do so today through the Privacy Act. Out of this desperation has grown a grassroots movement to help the war children find their roots in Canada. Project Roots has led the call to open veterans' files since 1980, when it was founded by Canadian veteran Lloyd Rains and his wife Olga, a Dutch war bride. Now it its twenty-fifth year, Project Roots has located and reunited more than 3,500 Canadian veterans with their children overseas. The Rains have authored three books: one about Olga's experience as a Canadian war bride, called *We Became Canadians*, and two about the Canadian war children, *Children of the Liberation* and *The Summer of 46*, which became the basis for a nine-part miniseries called *The Summer of 1945* (a Canadian-Dutch co-production). The Rains were honoured for their work with the Dutch war children in 1997, when Olga was awarded the Cross of Knighthood by Queen Beatrix of Holland.

For many years, the Rains used old-fashioned shoe-leather techniques to track down Canadian fathers and reunite them with their children, but in 1999, they made the leap onto the Internet and established a website (http://www.project-roots.com). The site contains hundreds of stories of war children searching for their Canadian fathers, many with photographs of the missing men dating back to the war years. Through the site, the Rains have been largely successful in locating dozens of veterans from their "Hard to Find" file. These cases would otherwise have remained unsolved had it not been for the Internet; the website has become a major tool in their searches.

The Rains get little or no help from Canadian government authorities who, citing the Privacy Act, turn a deaf ear to the plight of the war children. And although the *Canadian Legion Magazine* has relented somewhat in the past two or three years and redirected some inquiries about lost fathers to Project Roots, its practice has usually been to say no. Modern technology is up against them, however. The bulletin board on the Legion's new website is full of inquiries from war children about Canadian fathers.

Melynda Jarratt and Olga and Lloyd Rains at their first meeting in Fredericton, New Brunswick, September 1999. The three corresponded by letter, telephone and e-mail for more than five years before meeting face to face.

Olga Rains says the Privacy Act is the single biggest obstacle to tracing Canadian fathers, and it's incongruous with current attitudes towards unwed pregnancy, single mothers and their children which have shaped modern social policy. Citing recent federal legislation which purports to deal with parents and their responsibilities to children after a relationship breaks down, she says that the Canadian government has to make up its mind about the way it treats Canadians "by virtue of their service or not!"

Olga calls Canada's treatment of its war children a contradiction in values that debases the serviceman, whose most admirable quality was his heroism and obedience to orders. Calling parenthood the "ultimate responsibility," Olga hopes that more veteran fathers and their families will start owning up to the past, instead of trying to cover it up.

"That old way of thinking is hardly defensible today," Olga explains, "but many veterans continue to hide behind it, preferring to take their secret to the grave."

One need only read the death notices printed in any Canadian newspaper to see that thousands of World War II veterans are dying every year. As each day passes, the search for fathers becomes more urgent. Project Roots has met with members of Parliament and lobbied the privacy commissioner to open up veterans' files before the fathers have passed away, but without success.

The Canadian war children can find some solace in knowing they are not alone in their search for war fathers.[12] In Britain, the late Pamela Winfield established an organization called TRACE (Transatlantic Children's Enterprise), which helps the children of American GIs find their fathers in the United States.

TRACE has a website (http://www.tracepw.org) that contains search stories, photographs and information about how to trace an American GI father. Winfield authored four books, including one about her experiences as a GI bride, *Sentimental Journey*; and two about the GI children, *Melancholy Baby* and *Bye Bye Baby*. As a result of her tireless efforts to help the British children of American GIs, she was appointed an MBE by Queen Elizabeth II in January 2004. After a long illness, Pamela Winfield passed away in October 2004, but the organization she founded lives on.

As Winfield explained in the preface to this book, in 1984, a landmark case in the U.S. led to the limited opening of files for the children of GIs: "As long as they had basic information like a full name, and dates their fathers were in the U.K., these people were entitled to his last known address."

Taking it one step further, in 1989, a British organization called War Babes — established in the 1980s by GI war child Shirley McGlade — filed a class-action suit against the U.S. Defense Department, which was still refusing to release information about GI fathers. McGlade, who found her father in 1986, contended that the department was violating the U.S. Freedom to Information Act, and in November 1990, after much wrangling, the suit was settled. The results of the settlement are as follows:

1. The National Personnel Records Center (NPRC) will follow specified search procedures to look for records when a request for information about a veteran from War Babes or "similarly situated individual" is received.
2. The NPRC and Department of Defense (DOD) agree to disclose the city and state and date of whatever addresses are contained in the records of the GI being sought (if he is deceased, they will release the entire address) and;
3. For members of War Babes or World War II children, the NPRC will forward a letter on your behalf to your father by certified mail, return receipt requested (meaning it will only be delivered if your father signs for it).[13]

The precedent has also been set in Norway, where the *Krigsbarn* (war children of German servicemen stationed in Norway during World War II) have been granted access to information about their biological parents in the Lebensborn archives left behind by the departing Germans in 1945.[14]

The *Krigsbarn* were the result of love affairs — some serious, some fleeting — between the occupying German soldiers and Norwegian women, encouraged by the assistance offered to single unwed mothers through the Lebensborn maternity homes.[15] Mere toddlers and infants when the war ended, the *Krigsbarn* and their mothers were ostracized by Norwegian society, their lives marked by cruelty and hatred. Many *Krigsbarn* were given up for adoption, while others were institutionalized as mental defectives. As a group, they were treated with derision by a population that saw them as the children of the enemy, quislings who were an unwanted reminder of five terrible years of German occupation.

The most famous Norwegian war child is Frida Lyngstad, member of the world-famous pop group Abba, whose story of being reunited with her German father was explored in the BBC2 documentary film

Our Genes (2002). Frida's mother died soon after the war, and she was raised by her grandmother. When life became too difficult in their small village, Frida and her grandmother moved to Sweden, where Frida's musical career catupulted her to fame in the 1970s.

The Norwegian war-child organization Norges Krigbarforbund (NKBF) lobbied for access to the Lebensborn archives for many years while trying to raise awareness of the *Krigsbarn*'s unjust treatment after the war and their search for their biological parents. In 1986, Norwegian legislators passed a law that gave adoptees access to their adoption files, but it was not until 1994 that the *Krigsbarn* were finally able to see the Lebensborn archives in Norway's possession. Within the archives' 8,020 files could be found the names of their Norwegian mothers and German fathers, which they had been denied for nearly fifty years. In so doing, Norway has become the only Western country we are aware of that has opened up access to the files of its war children.

It is also the only country which has officially apologized for its treatment of war children in the postwar years. In a televised speech to the nation on January 1, 2000, Prime Minister Kjell Magne Bondevik acknowledged the suffering of the *Krigsbarn* and apologized for their discriminatory treatment at the hands of the authorities since the end of World War II.

In Norway, there is a small but impressive body of scholarship on the *Krigsbarn* authored by academics, scholars, advocates and war children themselves. At the same time, an organization called The War and Children Identity Project, based in Bergen, focuses on war children who were born of both enemy and Allied soldiers, including peacekeepers.[17] The organization grew partly out of the NKBF's movement to reunite war children with their biological parents, but also out of a growing recognition that there were other war children facing the same obstacles and discriminatory treatment all over the world.

The War and Children Identity Project has laudable goals and has produced the most comprehensive reports on the state of the world's war children that we have ever seen. War Children of the World 2001, 2002 and 2003[17] are valuable resources if for no other reason than for the questions they raise about social policy during and after war and the prejudice it breeds against these unfortunate children and their mothers. The 2001 report goes as far as to call for government to be held responsible for "hiding their employees from their offspring"[18] vis-à-vis privacy legislation that prevents access to a veteran's files long after he is dead, as is the case in Canada.

The War Children and Identity Project has the financial support of the Bergen city council to undertake its advocacy work — something we could only dream of in Canada. The organization is based on Section 7 of the United Nations Convention of the Rights of the Child, which holds that every child has a right to preserve his identity and family relations and to know his parents.[19] Its aims are:

- to secure the rights of war children to know about their parents;
- to secure children their right to nationality and identity;
- to secure children freedom from infringement of their rights based on their biological background; and
- to work equally for all war children born under war and warlike situations.

The organization's website (http://www.warandchildren.org) features research reports, oral histories and biographies that reveal that the problems facing war children are global in scope. It also lists a bibliography of work on the subject, extending beyond 1945 to include more recent wars, including Vietnam, Rwanda, Liberia, Sri Lanka and Bosnia, to name but a few.

In Britain, too, there are the home children, orphans and the poor, who were transported from the U.K. to Canada, Australia and New Zealand by more than fifty welfare organizations, including the Barnardo Homes, between 1870 and 1949. The Canadian home children suffered abuse and neglect as indentured farm labourers and domestic servants all over Canada. In 1998, a British parliamentary committee [20] unveiled a set of recommendations that, if fully implemented, could lead to family reunions. But for many home children, it was too late. Even if the agencies that brought them here so long ago co-operated — and many will not — their parents have long since died and relatives in Britain are scattered to the wind. For the home children, as for the Canadian war children whose fathers are located by Project Roots after he has passed away, all that is left of their identity is a grave across the Atlantic and the enduring mystery of who their parents really were.

NOTES

1. On December 9, 1946, on his last day as Minister of National Defence, Hon. D.C. Abbott presented a report on the "Problems Related to Wives and Dependents Residing Overseas," which included the problems presented by unwed mothers and their illegitimate children. Hon. D.C. Abbott, Minister of National Defence, to the Chairman, Cabinet

Committee on Demobilization and Re-Establishment, Immigration Branch. PAC, RG 76 Vol 462, File 705870, pt. 9.

2. These figures are estimates of Canadian war children in Britain and the Netherlands. Recent correspondence with the Public Records Office, the National Archives and the Office of National Statistics in the U.K., as well as the Dutch National Bureau of Statistics, the Ryks Instituut Oorlogs Documentatie (RIOD) and the Bureau Monumenten & Archeologie in Amsterdam confirm that evidence of Canadian paternity found in the birth certificates for illegitimate children born during the war years has never been compiled and is therefore unavailable at this time. It has also been suggested that the number of children whose fathers were Canadian servicemen may never be known, as married women whose British or Dutch husbands were away during the war would have given their Canadian children their husband's name as opposed to the biological father's name. We know this to be the case for several children whose stories appear in this book. The lack of readily available statistical evidence points to a need for further research in the archives of the respective countries to determine through objective analysis the numbers of war children whose fathers were Canadian servicemen.

3. "Wives who have signified their unwillingness to come to Canada are in most cases unwilling because their marriages have not been successful." Hon. D.C. Abbott, Minister of National Defence, to the Chairman, Cabinet Committee on Demobilization and Re-Establishment, Immigration Branch. PAC, RG 76 Vol 462, File 705870, pt. 9.

4. M.A. Robertson, High Commissioner, April 1, 1947, Immigration Branch. PAC, RG 76, Vol 462 File 705870, pt.10.

5. Letter from George Gillespie to Ralph Maybank MP, July 3, 1947. In his response some days later, Maybank assured Gillespie that not a single unwed mother with children had been allowed into Canada.

6. Colonel Ellis notes that this information was obtained "unofficially" and is of interest in considering the whole problem of servicemen's dependents. Movement and Welfare of Servicemen's Dependents after Disbandment of CWB, by Colonel George Ellis, Director of Repatriation, HQS 8536-1, PD [Repat]. November 9, 1946.

7. A survey by the author of leading Canadian military historians and sociologists in the summer of 2003 found that there has been little, if any, research done on the subject of child support for the children, illegitimate or legitimate, of Canadian servicemen who served overseas during World War II.

8. M.A. Robertson, High Commissioner, April 1, 1947, Immigration Branch. PAC, RG 76, Vol 462 File 705870, pt.10.

9. Ibid.

10. Interview with the author, September 2000.

11. Ruth Roach Pierson, *They're Still Women After All: The Second World War and Canadian Womanhood* (Toronto: McClelland & Stewart, 1986).

12. Jenel Virden has written about the issue of the illegitimate children of American GIs in her study of British war brides who married U.S. soldiers during World War II, *Goodbye Picadilly: British War Brides in America* (1996). Virden is a lecturer in the Department of American Studies at the University of Hull, England, and is the daughter of a war bride. In the chapter "Transatlantic Divorce, Paternity, and Incomplete Immigration," she cites extensive archival sources to document the hauntingly similar experiences of British women who bore the children of American GIs out of wedlock. Attempts by mothers to obtain child support for their children, or in cases where the women were married, alimony and child support from their GI ex-husbands, as well as the war children's efforts to find a U.S. soldier since the end of the war, mirror the Canadian experience.

13. Information about the War Babes class-action suit is on the website (http://www.gitraceorg/warbabes.htm).

14. Thanks to Joakim Ophaug and Elna Johnson of The War Children and Identity Project for their assistance in providing information about the history of the *Krigsbarn*, the Norges Krigsbarnforbund (NKBF) and the Lebensborn maternity homes.

15. Although the Lebensborn archives document 8,020 cases of *Krigsbarn*, it is estimated that 12,000 war children were born of unions between Norwegian women and German servicemen during and immediately after World War II. Joakim Ophaug and Elna Johnson of The War and Children Identity Project estimate that another 2,000 were born in 1945 for which records are unavailable. They say there were likely another 2,000 *Krigsbarn* born in 1946, but the exact number will probably never be known.

16. The War Children and Identity Project is located in Bergen, Norway, and has a website (http://www.warandchildren.org) where its history, mandate, goals and major research reports can be found. The organization has the financial support of the city council of Bergen, Norway to carry out its advocacy work.

17. The War Children of the World, Report 1, December 2001, by Kai Greig, published by War Children and Identity Project, Bergen, Norway, ISBN 82-996703-0-6, and The War Children of the World Report 2, 2002, by Bard Kartveit, published by War and Children Identity Project, Bergen, Norway, ISBN 82-996703-1-4.

War Children of the World Report 3, 2003, by Joakim Ophaug (ed.), published by War and Children Identity Project, Bergen, Norway, ISBN 82-996703-2-2.

18. The War Children of the World, Report 1, December 2001, by Kai Greig, p. 14.

19. The UN Convention on the Rights of the Child can be viewed online at http://www.unhcr.ch/html/menu3/b/k2crc.htm. Canada is a signatory to the UN Convention on the Rights of the Child and as such is obligated to live up to its standards.

20. United Kingdom Parliament, The Select Committee on Health, Third Report, The Welfare Of Former British Child Migrants, http://www.parliament.the-stationery-office.co.uk/pa/cm199798/cmselect/cmhealth/755/75513.htm.

Appendix

Correspondence

* indicates where names have been changed

Letter from Louis Burwell, January 1, 1941

Note: This was a letter written to my mother, Sheila, from my father, Louis Burwell, when he was stationed in England with the Canadian Army. They would get married in February 1942. — Bob Burwell

Dearest one,

This is the third letter I've started today, surely this time I can make it sound half-way decent, what a horrible start to the New Year! How are you sweetheart, I do hope you are feeling much better today, indeed lately I'm most depressed, now realising just what you are going through. Sheila, my mind has ever since been in a turmoil. I cannot think clearly, don't know what to do. But I beg you to hear me out.

What I thought was merely some ailment you were suffering from is now evidently a purely mental state. I can now see that our relationship has become vitally important to both of us. Sadly it seems, but you've fallen for the one who is severely handicapped and I'm completely at sea. What are we to do?

I finally came to the decision that I led you into this tangle and it's my job to lead you out of it as gently as possible. Darling you must see things from my point of view. Could I possibly help you to build some beautiful castle and then bring the whole thing tumbling down upon yourself, all in ruins? What effect would that have upon your life afterwards?

Such a lovely young life — surely I must not be the one to break your little heart? Love is never hidden from the world, it is such a beautiful, clean thing — a gift for all to gaze upon — yet we must keep silent. I see questioning eyes — they look accusingly at me and say — how can you take this girls' feelings so lightly. I see you digging into your little savings, scratching along with what is left of your salary, so many things you deny yourself in order to be along with me. Darling it is intolerable — we simply cannot continue. I've tried to be offensive, disagreeable and unkind. Always you come up smiling and I see the hurt expression I dread so much to witness. But it is not wrong to love truly and I'm responsible for encouraging you when all I had to do was act indifferently towards you and just be as I intended, a very good friend towards you. I love you, I need you, my life would have one big empty space without you.

Leaving you would be just like taking the sun away and I'd be ever-lastingly groping in perpetual darkness. You've just become part of me. I've had happiness I'm sure no one else could have had — such lovely days — always ours alone. After all you are different from the usual type one meets here. I was gazing at your photo after tea, Robinson looks at it and says — "Will you show your wife that picture?" Golly, I was taken aback!

I simply replied "Why sure, why not, that's a swell kid!" But of course he would not understand, no one would. We must do the right thing — not because we consider others — simply because we could not do otherwise. Is the mere possibility of some future life with me going to be worth all that? Are we big enough to see it through? Some may suggest that we just meander along until we reach the parting of our ways and then calmly proceed along our own paths. But that could not be because we'd never manage it and both of us would fall so badly and we'd not have the comfort of each other's assistance. The other solution is a clean break and sum it all up by saying we did love and live, so let's forget it. Then what?

Which leaves only the inevitable way open — divorce and shortly after that sheer possibility — our marriage. It is the only way, no other will suffice. As far as all those I knew before are concerned, they'd just have to accept it the same way as if I just died and they were receiving a pension. How horrible all that sounds, but it is the only way.

Sheila, we have got a terrible tiger by the tail — and you're so darn swell and good and kind and loveable — what a future to look forward to. Sweetheart, this is the most horrible letter I've ever written in my life, and to the finest little girl I could ever wish to meet. All I ask now is that you burn this letter and I'm relying on your understanding and kindness to do so, for me. You know I admire you, every darn thing about you — that I love you and care more and more for you with each passing day. Just look ahead a little and ask yourself is all that worth one man's love ?

Meanwhile Peaches and Cream — I'm thinking of you, need you always. I love you as much as it is possible for me to love. So until Saturday night, Goodnight dear heart.

God Bless and keep you well.
Always Yours alone,
Lou

Letter from Guildford Rural District Council, Billeting Department, March 22, 1943

My dear Prence,

I have been seriously thinking over the matter which we discussed on Saturday afternoon, when I told you of the number of babies of Canadian soldiers we are asked to find homes for.

I think your suggestion that some sort of a fund should be started, and I do fully appreciate the fact that it should not be given any official status. I was wondering therefore, whether it could not be made part of some general scheme.

I do not know if you are aware of the fact that there is in this country a very excellent organisation known as the Soldiers, Sailors & Airman's Families Association, and I am rather wondering whether the time has not come for a similar organisation to be set up for the wives and families of Canadian soldiers in this country. If this was done, it would be perfectly legitimate to help out of the Association's funds any cases of illegitimate children.

I only put this suggestion forward for what it is worth, and you may not consider it a good idea, but…

James

Letter from Immigration Branch, Department of Mines and Resources, London, England, to Miss Maria Franzen, Klies, Birkenfeld, Germany, November 8, 1946

Dear Madam:

I am advised by the Director of the Immigration at Ottawa that your fiancé Mr. Leslie Barden has made application for your admission to Canada, and that the settlement arrangements are satisfactory. It is noted there is an expected child, which will be included.

It is regretted, however, that owing to the lack of transportation between the Continent of Europe and Canada, no action can be taken for the present, but, as soon as conditions become more normal, our

Canadian Immigration Inspectional Service will be established again on the Continent of Europe, when your case will be dealt with.

You can rely on being advised when our Continental Offices have re-opened, and I would ask that your refrain from making further enquiries in the matter in the meantime.

Your fiancé has been advised by the Director of Immigration at Ottawa that there may be delay in your proposed movement to Canada.

Yours faithfully
O.S.
For Commissioner

Letter from Immigration Branch, Department of Mines and Resources, London, to Miss Maria Franzen, March 3, 1947

Dear Madam:

On the 8th November, 1946, I advised you that settlement arrangements were satifactory for you and your expected child with your fiancé, Leslie Barden of 2249 Girouard Avenue, Montreal P.Q.

I would now inform you that a communication has been received from our Departmental Authorities in Canada, to the effect that your fiancé wishes further action in your case to be deferred, as he is unable to assume any obligations at the present time.

In view of the foregoing, settlement arrangements can no longer be considered satisfactory for you and your child, and the Department's approval for your admission to our Dominion is withdrawn.

Kindly return to this office as soon as possible our aforementioned letter of November 8th last.

Yours faithfully
K.B
For Commissioner

Letter from Immigration Branch, Department of Mines and Resources, London, to Miss Maria Franzen, May 21, 1947

Dear Madam:

On November 8th, 1946, I advised you that settlement arrangements were satisfactory for you and your expected child at the home of your fiancé, Mr. Leslie Barden of 2249 Girouard Avenue, Montreal, P.Q., and that your entry was approved subject to health requirements, and making your own transportation arrangements.

I am now in receipt of a letter from the Director of the Immigration at Ottawa, stating that your fiancé has advised the department that he wishes his application for your admission to Canada to be cancelled. In view of this, the settlement arrangements are no longer considered satisfactory and we are unable to deal further with your application for admission to Canada. Will you, therefore, kindly return to this office for cancellation our letter mentioned above of the 8th November 1946.

Yours faithfully
O.S.
For Commissioner

Letter from Immigration Branch, Department of Mines and Resources, Regina, Saskatchewan, to MacIain MacGregor* of Saskatchewan, October 16, 1947

Dear Sir:

With reference to your application for the admission to Canada of Miss Geertje Johanna Valderviken,* and her child, Gesina Petronella,* citizens of Holland presently residing at Manege Straat 7, Haarlem,* C. Holland, you are informed that the above named do not come within the category of relationships provided for under present immigration regulations, and it is therefore regretted that no further action can be taken with a view to authorising their admission to Canada at the present time.

Yours truly
DN
Inspector-in-Charge

Letter from Department of Veterans Affairs, Ottawa, to Mrs. Scholten* of The Netherlands, September 26, 1956

Re: Charles Smith*

Dear Madam:

Replying to your letter of September 9th, it must be stated that it is contrary to the Regulations of the Department to release any information regarding veterans without their consent.

This could not be obtained in the case about which you have written as the whereabouts of the veteran is unknown.

Yours very truly
H.M
Chief Executive Assistant

Letter from lawyer JMR,* Fredericton, New Brunswick, to Lloyd and Olga Rains, January 18, 1991

Dear Mr. and Mrs. Rains:

Re: Morton Haley*

As you may understand, the news of a new member of the family being a possibility has been a bit of an upset. Mrs. Haley* is the most concerned and this has affected Morton.

He requested that I write to you and request that you not write or phone anymore. His health has been poor lately and he was not prepared for this intrusion into his life.

He and my father were friends, both veterans and both stationed in England during the war, so I am not unaware of your client's situation. I did, however, urge Mr. Haley to write and at least make contact even though he doubts the lady is his daughter. He may or may not be but I would request that you make no further phone calls and leave the rest to Mr. Haley and Mrs. Whalen.*

Yours truly,
JMR*

Letter from Lloyd and Olga Rains to lawyer JMR,* January 28, 1991

Dear JMR:*

We received your letter regarding Morton Haley.*

I would like to explain that we are not an organization, are not supported by anyone or any country or any other organization. Therefore, Mrs. Whalen* is not our client.

Carol Whalen came to us and asked us to help her find her biological father, who is Mr. Morton Haley.*

Mr. Haley and Carol's mother, Helen Eunice Underhill,* knew each other for one and a half years and he was aware that he was going to be a father.

He wrote to Carol's mother twice, once before and once after she was born. In his second letter he asked: "You might as well tell me what sex it is."

Carol was conceived in April of 1944 and was born January 10, 1945. Shortly after her birth, her mother was told by one of Morton's senior officers that Morton and his friend Joe both had been killed in Germany. There is no record of that, we did research. That was a very common procedure in those days [to make up stories about the Canadian soldier], as the officers had to protect their men. As soon as a soldier got a girl pregnant and he wanted "out," he was able to get a transfer right away. We have heard hundreds of those stories over the last 10 years.

Carol's mother really loved Morton and she became very upset and withdrawn. She was a nurse at the time she met Morton in Bristol. Carol was raised by her grandparents, it was them who gave her the photo of Morton and Joe. Her mother got married later on, but her husband did not want Carol.

Today Carol is a trained psychiatric nurse. She married when she was 18 and is still happily married. They have a son who is studying for his PhD, he is 26. Carol also has a daughter who is a nurse and is 20.

Carol does not need the love of a father anymore now, she just wants to know her roots in Canada. We think she has the God given right like every one else has. That is the least that Morton can give her now, he never contributed any support for her at all, like so many other soldiers did while in England after they got a girl pregnant.

I realize this must have been a shock for Morton after so many years. He does not have to worry about having to pay any money.

219

So far we have reunited more than 800 Canadian fathers with their offspring, or as some Canadians call them "War Leftovers."

It is unbelievable that after so many years these "war children" still have to be a secret in Canada. We are glad there not many like Morton, most fathers will accept their "child". They are richer for it and as many put it in words like; "Well, the past has finally caught up with me."

I do not know if Morton had children, if he does, we think they should know about their half-sister in England. In ten years we have seen so much happiness and friendship between the veteran's Canadian children and the warchild and they are all richer for it. The younger generation like yourself doesn't think anything of it and they do not care what Daddy did in England, Holland, Belgium and so on.

In this case we will not try and contact Morton's family and we will not contact him anymore. It is a pity that Mrs. Haley cannot be informed properly of what war was like and what happened over there. I do understand that is must be hard for her. Most wives of the veterans are willing to talk to us and ask many questions about that time. We go and see them in person if we can. We have travelled throughout Canada twice and also visited many veterans and their wives in your area.

Also she is missing out on a beautiful happening in her life. Most veteran's wives are the ones who wait at the airports with open arms and loving hearts to welcome their husband's war baby.

Carol is coming to Canada in March, so she told me. She had hoped to meet her father once and look into his eyes and shake his hand. She has no bitter feelings toward him, she understands. I am sure that she will respect his wishes and leave him alone.

Who knows, maybe Morton will change his mind. He has to live with it and that will not improve his health any, nor that of his wife.

Some veterans would rather live with the turmoil, because they are too ashamed of what they have done.

I am writing you this long letter because I hope that you will help Morton or find someone who will, like the Minister of his church or his doctor. Over the years doctors and Ministers have played a helping role in our Project and have been able to bring father and child together.

Enclosed find a few stories about our project.

Thank you for reading this long letter.

Sincerely
Lloyd and Olga Rains

Letter from Mr. Mackie,* lawyer, Ottawa, to Linda Tucker,* July 9, 1991

Dear Mrs. Linda Tucker,*

Please be advised that I represent Mr. John Barker.*

My client has brought me photocopies of the correspondence that has been received from you between March of this year and the current date. I note that you believe that my client is your father and that you wish him to admit this to you in order that you may feel some ease on this issue.

My client denies that he is your father. I have advised him that the law of Ontario (which is similar to the law of England) places no obligation on him to prove or disprove your allegations. There are no legal obligations upon a putative father for a child who is no longer dependant or a minor. In a situation where paternity is alleged but not proven, our courts have the jurisdiction to order blood tests in order that the right of the child to support may be addressed. Neither of these rights nor obligations exists in this situation and our law does not take an interest in the emotional satisfaction which is admittedly of importance to you.

Further, I have advised my client that blood tests themselves are inconclusive for a small percentage of the population. There may be, therefore, no scientific way of eliminating my client from the class of men who may be your father.

Please accept this letter as a request that all future contact between yourself, your children, and my client cease. The letters that you have received from Mrs. John Barker state most strongly that my client's health, the well being of his marriage, and the health of his wife of 45 years have been adversely affected by this experience. My client shall respond to no further communications and I have instructed him to return all mail that he receives from you to you. I trust that this satisfies your questions.

Your truly,
Mr. Mackie* (lawyer for Mr. John Barker)

Letter from Olga Rains to lawyer Mark Sloan,* Halifax, April 22, 1992

Dear Sir:

In answer to your letter dated April 10th, 1992, we are not an organization and are not supported by anyone. Therefore Mr. Jack Gordon's* son is not our client. He is one of the thousands of war babies left behind by our servicemen after World War Two. We help these war victims find their biological fathers in Canada.

Mr. Jack Gordon has known for years that he had a son in England. He should have known that someday the past would catch up with him! He fathered a child, left it behind in England and now he wants to brush him out of his life completely.

I do not feel responsible for the state of Mr. Gordon's health. I made one phone call to him and when I mentioned the name Annie, the mother of his son, he hung up on me. After that I wrote him a letter which he sent to you.

I will honour his wishes and will not contact him or his family. He wants to be left in peace. I wonder if that is possible for him for all he has on his conscience.

Sincerely
Olga Rains

Letter from Personnel Records Unit, National Archives of Canada, Ottawa, to Mr. Van Driest* of The Netherlands, January 7, 1993

Re: Warren Hamilton*

Dear Sir:

This refers to your letter, in which you request the last known address of the above named ex-serviceperson.

In accordance with the Privacy Act we are not permitted to disclose this information to a third party. In cases where the ex-serviceperson can be positively identified, we may offer to forward a letter to him, but as he has not communicated with the department since his discharge from the Canadian Armed Forces, his present whereabouts is unknown.

It is regretted that we cannot be of greater assistance to you in this matter.

Sincerely
H.T.
Public Inquiries Correspondent
Personnel Records Unit
Researcher Services Division

Letter from Research and Public Affairs Enquiries Officer, National Archives of Canada, to Donna Barkhouse* of Winchester, Hants, England, November 20, 1994

Dear Madam

Re: Mr. Salsbury*

This refers to your recent inquiry, in which you request information concerning Mrs. Salsbury,* the wife of the above named.

May we explain, that in accordance with the stipulations of the Privacy Act, we are forbidden by law to release to a third party the whereabouts of an individual without the consent of the subject individual.

When a person is identified, under certain circumstances this office will attempt to contact him/her in order to inform him/her of the inquiry we have received.

In the case of Mrs. Salsbury, we wish to inform you that we wrote to her on October 17, 1994, requesting that she communicate with this office so that we could discuss a personal matter which had been brought to our attention (your enquiry).

She telephoned us on November 9, 1994, and she was told the nature of your letter. However, she has requested that her whereabouts be kept confidential as she did not wish to establish contact with you, nor did she wish the matter pursued any further by our department.

We might add that Mrs. Salsbury informed us that Mr. Salsbury died on January 20, 1992. For the foregoing reasons, we regret that we can not be of further assistance to you. Your letter will be placed in her late husband's file.

Sincerely
M.K., Research and Public Enquiries Officer

Letter from Personnel Records Unit, National Archives of Canada, to Carol Packard* of Winchester, Hants, England, December 20, 1994

Dear Madam:

Re: John Arnold Gauthier,* husband of Joanne Darlene Gauthier*

This refers to your recent inquiry in which you request information about Mrs. Gauthier, the wife of the above named. May we explain, that in accordance with the stipulations of the Privacy Act, we are forbidden by law to release to a third party the whereabouts of an individual without the consent of the subject individual. When a person is identified, under certain circumstances this office will attempt to contact him / her in order to inform him / her of the inquiry we have received.

In the case of Mrs. Gauthier, we wish to inform you that we wrote to her on 23 November 1994, requesting that she communicate with this office so that we could discuss with her a personal matter which had been brought to our attention (i.e. your inquiry). She telephoned us on 19 December and she was told the nature of your letter. However, she has requested that her whereabouts be kept confidential as she did not want to establish contact with you, nor did she wish the matter pursued any further by our department. We might add that, Mrs. Gauthier advised us that John Arnold Gauthier died on 14 June 1994.

For the foregoing reasons, although we can appreciate your interest in contacting Mrs. Gauthier or learning more about her, regretfully we can be of no further assistance to you. Your letter has, however, been placed in her late husband's file for any future reference.

Sincerely,
C.L.

Research and Public Inquiries Officer
Personnel Records Unit
Researcher Services Division

Letter from Inquiries Officer, Office of the Privacy Commissioner of Canada, to Melynda Jarratt, May 7, 2001

Dear Ms. Jarratt:

I am writing to you further to your email dated April 3, 2001 regarding the children of WWII veterans and access to their fathers' military records. Please accept my apologies for the delay in responding to your inquiry.

You asked several questions on this issue, and I will do my best to provide you with all the relevant information.

The definition of personal information can be found in section 2 of the Privacy Act. This definition is quite comprehensive, and its intent is to define what is, and what is not, personal information. Section 2 (m) is most relevant to your query. It states that for the purposes of sections 7, 8 and 26 of the Privacy Act and section 19 of the Access to Information Act, personal information does not include information about an individual who has been dead for more than twenty years. Also, section 26 of the Privacy Act states that the head of a government institution may refuse to disclose any personal information about an individual other than the individual who made the request, and shall refuse to disclose such information where the disclosure is prohibited under section 8.

Furthermore, you asked whether the practice of protecting personal information under the Privacy Act in this manner is the same with today's soldiers as it is with the soldiers of WWII. The Privacy Act has been in existence since 1983 and applies to all personal information under the control of a federal government institution. Therefore, the personal information of a soldier actively serving in the military would be granted the same level of protection as that of his predecessors, as long as it is under the control of a federal government institution subject to the Act.

In addition, you wanted to know what privacy legislation prevents British and European children of WWII veterans whose parents were not married from accessing their fathers military personnel files. The right to request information under both the Privacy Act and the Access to Information Act is limited to Canadian citizens and permanent residents within the meaning of the Immigration Act, inmates in federal penitentiaries, and all persons present in Canada. Also, proof of the individuals death and proof of the relationship to the deceased individual must be provided in order to request information under both these Acts.

Finally, you asked why it is that National Archives current policies deny the children of WWII veterans access to their fathers personal information, and thus allow these veterans to hide from their children. We are sympathetic to the plight of those whose access rights may be limited by the restrictions imposed by the Privacy Act. However, the Office of the Privacy Commissioner does not have the authority to compel National Archives of Canada, nor any other federal government institution, to release or withhold information. I suggest that you pursue this inquiry with your Member of Parliament, the Minister of Canadian Heritage, or the Department of Justice.

The Minister of Canadian Heritage, the Honourable Sheila Copps, is responsible for implementing policies regarding the National Archives of Canada. You may write to the Minister at 509 S Centre Block Building, Ottawa, Ontario, K1A 0A6.

Furthermore, the Public Law Policy section of the Department of Justice is in the process of drafting proposed reforms to the existing Privacy Act. You may forward your concerns about the legislation in writing at 284 Wellington Street, Ottawa, Ontario, K1A 0H8.

The Privacy Commissioner is a specialist ombudsman appointed by and accountable to Parliament who monitors the federal governments collection, use, and disclosure of its clients and employees personal information, and its handling of individuals requests to see their records. This office investigates complaints on behalf of individuals who feel they have been denied their rights under the Privacy Act.

I trust that I have adequately addressed your inquiry. Please contact me at 1-800-282-1376 should you have any further questions.

Sincerely,
Anne Blais
Inquiries Officer

Letter from Personnel Records Unit, National Archives of Canada, to Olga Rains, November 25, 2003

Dear Madam:

Re: Oliver Jackson*

In reply to your request concerning the above named, please note that in accordance with the Privacy Act, access to records or release of personal information relating to an individual is not permitted without the written consent of the individual concerned. In the event that the individual has been dead for less than 20 years, limited information may be released directly to members of the immediate family, if proof of death (death certificate, obituary notice, etc.) and proof of relationship (baptismal certificate, marriage certificate or any other document that clearly demonstrates the relationship) are provided. A wallet-sized birth certificate which does not state the parent's name is not accepted as proof of relationship. There are no restrictions placed on information relating to a person who has been dead for more than 20 years, however, proof of death is still required.

Accordingly, as he has been deceased for less than 20 years, personal information from Mr. Jackson's military file can only be released to a member of his immediate family, upon receipt of written request and proof of relationship.

Sincerely,
B.S.
Personnel Records Officer
Personnel Records Unit
Researcher Services Division

Letter from Syd Frost, Commanding Officer, Princess Patricia's Canadian Light Infantry

Lloyd and Olga Rains are well known throughout Holland as the originators of Project Roots, a voluntary agency that has reunited more than 3,500 Canadian Veterans with the war children they left behind in Europe at the end of World War Two.

Olga is a Dutch war bride who met Lloyd during the Dutch Liberation in 1945. Lloyd is No. B68601 Private L. V. Rains who joined the PPCLI on February 14, 1945, and was a member of my D Company during the crossing of the Yssel River and subsequent operations.

The Rains lived in Canada for 50 years and then returned to Holland where they now reside and carry on their work. In April 1997, Olga was awarded the Cross of Knighthood by Queen Beatrix.

Lloyd and Olga have also been active on behalf of the Patricia's, not only during the Pilgrimages, but also in the intervening years.

When the "Second Battle" of the crossing of the Yssel River erupted, as to which Regiment was involved, the Rains gave their full support to the PPCLI.

When the smoke cleared and our claim to the honour had been rightfully restored, the Rains arranged for an additional Memorial to be added to the exisiting monument on the west bank of the Yssel River at Gorssel by the Canadian Army on April 12th, 1945, when the liberation of western Holland began.

The memorial added by Lloyd and Olga Rains makes it very clear who did the job.

PPCLI
PRINCESS PATRICIA'S CANADIAN LIGHT INFANTRY
FIRST REGIMENT TO CROSS THE YSSEL RIVER
12 APRIL, 1945

PPCLI
Commanding Officer Syd Frost

Bibliography

Books and Reports

Banister, Lisa. *Equal to the Challenge: An Anthology of Women's Experiences During World War II.* Ottawa: Department of National Defence, 2001.

Costello, John. *Love, Sex and War: Changing Values, 1939–45.* London: Collins, 1985.

Gaffen, Fred. *Forgotten Soldiers.* Penticton, B.C.: Theytus Books, 1985.

Granatstein, J.L., and Desmond Morton. *A Nation Forged in Fire.* Toronto: Lester & Orpen Dennys, 1989.

Greig, Kai. *The War Children of the World*, Report 1. Bergen, Norway: The War Children and Identity Project, 2001.

Jarratt, Melynda. "The War Brides of New Brunswick." Master's Thesis, University of New Brunswick, 1995.

Kartveit, Bard. *The War Children of the World*, Report 2. Bergen, Norway: The War and Children Identity Project, 2002.

Ophaug, Joakim. *The War Children of the World*, Report 3. Bergen, Norway: The War and Children Identity Project, 2003.

Piddiscombe, Perry, "Dangerous Liaisons: The Anti-Fraternization Movement in the U.S Occupation Zones of Germany and Austria, 1945–1948." *Journal of Social History*, June 2001.

Pierson, Ruth Roach. *They're Still Women after All: The Second World War and Canadian Womanhood.* Toronto: McClelland and Stewart, 1986.

Prentice, Alison, et al. *Canadian Women: A History*. Toronto: Harcourt Brace Jovanovich, 1988.

Rains, Olga. *Children of the Liberation*. Hyde Park, Ont.: Overnight Copy Service, 1985.

————. *The Summer of 46*. Hyde Park, Ont.: Overnight Copy Service, 1988.

————. *We Became Canadians*. Hyde Park, Ont.: Overnight Copy Service, 1984.

Royal Commission on Aboriginal Peoples. *Report of the Royal Commission on Aboriginal Peoples*. Ottawa: The Commission, 1996. (Available online at http://www.ainc-inac.gc.ca/ch/rcap/sg/sgmm_e.html)

Ryberg, Percy E. *Health, Sex and Birth Control*. Toronto: The Anchor Press, 1943.

A Search for Equality: National Roundtable Report, May 2001.

Summerby, Janice. *Native Soldiers, Foreign Battlefields*. Ottawa: Govt. of Canada, Veterans Affairs, 1993.

Virden, Jenel. *Good-bye Picadilly: British War Brides in America*. Urbana, Ill.: University of Illinois Press, 1996.

Winfield, Pamela. *Bye Bye Baby: The Story of the Children the GIs Left Behind*. London: Bloomsbury, 1992.

————. *Melancholy Baby: The Unplanned Consequences of the GIs' Arrival in Europe for World War II*. Greenwood Press. 2000.

————, and Brenda Hasty. *Sentimental Journey: The Story of the GI Brides*. London: Constable, 1984.

Websites

Canada's Digital Collections, "Courage Remembered: Native Veterans." Industry Canada. http://collections.ic.gc.ca/courage/nativeveterans.html

GI TRACE. http://www.gitrace.org

Krigsbarnforbundet Lebensborn (The League Lebensborn of Norwegian Children's of War). Home page. http://home.no.net/lebenorg/

Norges Krigsbarnforbund (Norwegian Children of War Association). Home page. http://www.nkbf.no

NS-Children: Children of Members of the National Unification (NS) in Norway. Home page. http://home.no.net/nsbarn/

Organization of Norwegian NS Children. Home page. http://home.online.no/~kluwer/ and http://www.nazichildren.org/

Project Roots. Home page. http://www.project-roots.com

Report of the Royal Commission on Aboriginal Peoples. Department of Indian and Northern Affairs. http://www.ainc-inac.gc.ca/ch/rcap/sg/sgmm_e.html

A Search for Equality: National Roundtable Report, May 2001. http://ourworld.compuserve.com/homepages/aboriginal/rndtable.htm

TRACE — Transatlantic Children's Enterprise. Home page. http://www.gitrace.org

United Nations High Commissioner for Human Rights. "Convention on the Rights of the Child." http://www.unhchr.ch/html/menu3/b/k2crc.htm

The War and Children Identity Project. Home page. http://www.warandchildren.org

Primary Sources

British Birth Statistics

Authors' correspondence with Public Records Office, UK, December 2003.

Authors' correspondence with the National Archives, UK, December 2003.

Authors' correspondence with the Office of National Statistics, UK, December 2003.

Dutch Birth Statistics

Authors' correspondence with the Dutch National Bureau of Statistics, December 2003.

Authors' correspondence with the Bureau Monumenten & Archeologie Amsterdam

Statistics Netherlands.

Norwegian Krigsbarn

Authors' correspondence with Joakim Ophaug and Elna Johnson of The War and Children Identity Project, December 2003, January 2004.

Canadian Wives Bureau, War Brides and Illegitimate Children

Public Archives of Canada

War Children

Authors' correspondence and interviews with: John, Sheila Blake, Alan Franklin, Celestine, Christine Wilson, Sandra Connor, Christine Coe, Robert Burwell, Jenny Moore, Peter Hurricks, Jill, Mary K., Pat K., Carol Anne Hobbs, Ralph Thompson, Karen Cockwell, Maureen Fletcher, Mira, Katja, Alma, Elly & Stan, Johnny Bruggenkamp, Mia, Hans Kingma, Theo Timmer, Nel, Leona Tange, Simonne Gallis, Richard Bond, Jan Walker, Diane, Eloise, Sally, Pamela Walker, Irene Lynk, Margaret Atkinson, Winnie Bullen, Peter, Kathleen Swann, Willy Joormans, Willy Van Ee, Josephine Gee, Joan Kramer-Potts, Chris, Nano Pennefeather-McConnell, Beverly Susanne Werth, Diane and Ron Matthews, Heiko Windels.

Photo Credits

Page 12. Lloyd and Olga Rains with Melynda Jarratt, September 2003. Source: Jan Walker.

Page 13. Pamela Winfield. Source: Pamela Winfield, as found in her book, *Bye Bye Baby*.

Chapter 1 The Canadians in Britain 1939–1946

Page 15. King George VI inspects the Canadian Highland Regiment (date unknown, circa World War II). Source: Ralph and Lois Thompson. *Note: This photo was known by the family of C.W. Thompson to be their father's personal photograph. It had the words WRIGHT RADIO SERVICE and PERFECT PICTURES on the back of the print. Every attempt was made to contact Wright Radio Service and Perfect Pictures to obtain permission to reproduce this photograph.*

Page 16. Friends and family celebrate the return of a Canadian serviceman from overseas. Source: Dan Weston.

Page 21. Gavin McGurk (or McGuire). Source: Sheila Blake.

Page 22. Sheila Blake with her mother, Patricia Ayling. Source: Sheila Blake.

Page 23. Alan Franklin. Source: Alan Franklin

Page 24. *Surrey-Hants Star*. Source: Alan Franklin.

Page 27. A Canadian soldier at a train station. Source: Olga and Lloyd Rains.

Page 30. Sheila Blake as a toddler. Source: Sheila Blake.

Page 34. Christine Wilson. Source: Christine Wilson

Page 36. Christine Wilson with her Canadian family. Source: Christine Wilson.

Page 37. War child with white dress. Source: Olga and Lloyd Rains.

Page 39. Harry Potter. Source: Christine E. Coe.

Page 40. Christine E. Coe. Source: Christine E. Coe.

Page 42. Louis Burwell. Source: Robert Burwell.

Page 44. Jenny Moore and her Canadian family. Source: Jenny Moore.

Page 45. Jack Neale. Source: Peter Hurricks.

Page 46. Peter Hurricks and his mother Agnes Hurricks. Source: Peter Hurricks.

Page 49. Jack Neale. Source: Peter Hurricks.

Page 50. Jill and her dog. Source: Jill.

Page 56. C.W. Thompson. Source: Ralph and Lois Thompson.

Page 58. Carol Anne Hobbs and Ralph Thompson. Source: Ralph and Lois Thompson.

Page 63. Maureen's father in uniform. Source: Maureen Fletcher.

Page 127. Army wife and baby on a Canadian Army base. Source: Dan Weston.

Page 129. A Canadian serviceman and his war bride. Source: Olga Rains.

Chapter 4 War Children Who Were Adopted

Page 135. Winnie Bullen's adoption file photos. Source: Winnie Bullen.

Page 138. Robert Cecil Martin. Source: Pamela Walker.

Page 141. Pamela Walker and grandson. Source: Pamela Walker.

Page 143. Mary Wetherhall, Margaret Atkinson's biological mother. Source: Margaret Atkinson.

Page 144. Margaret Atkinson. Source: Margaret Atkinson.

Page 145. Winnie Bullen. Source: Winnie Bullen.

Page 149. Winnie Bullen in a recent photo. Source: Winnie Bullen.

Page 152. Peter with his Canadian family. Source: Peter. *Note: This photograph and an article about Peter and his Canadian family appeared in the* Cape Breton Post *on April 5, 1997.*

Page 154. Kathleen Swann's father. Source: Kathleen Swann.

Page 155. Yvon Pelletier. Source: Willy Joormans.

Page 159. Willy Joormans with Canadian family: Source: Serge Ligtenberg of the Associated Press.

Chapter 5 Native Roots

Page 161. Willy van Ee's parents. Source: Willy van Ee.

Page 165. Lloyd and Olga Rains with Willy van Ee in his yard. Source: Lloyd Rains.

Page 166. Willy van Ee as toddler. Source: Willy van Ee.

Page 168. Donald Potts. Source: Josephine Gee.

Page 170. Josephine Gee as a little girl. Source: Josephine Gee.

Page 172. Josephine Gee and her half-brother, Roger Potts. Source: Josephine Gee.

Chapter 6 Children of Canadian Servicewomen

Page 175. Servicewomen and men dancing in England. Source: Nano Pennefeather-McConnell. *Note: The back of this photograph contains faded text which indicates copyright is owned by the Royal Canadian Air Force. There is also a file number on the front of the photograph HQ2099.*

The Authors

Lloyd and Olga Rains

Lloyd Rains is a Canadian veteran of World War II, having served in Italy and in Northwestern Europe as a member of Princess Patricia's Canadian Light Infantry (PPCLI). In the weeks following the Liberation of Holland in May 1945, Lloyd met Olga (née Trestorff). The young couple fell in love and married on Christmas Eve, 1945. After the war, Olga came to Canada as a war bride, and she and Lloyd settled in Ontario, where they raised a family, lived and worked for most of their married lives. In 1980, while on a return trip to Holland to attend celebrations of the thirty-fifth anniversary of the Dutch Liberation, they encountered some Dutch war children and thus was born Project Roots. Olga has authored three books, one about her experiences as a Canadian war bride, *We Became Canadians*, and two others about the Canadian war children called *Children of the Liberation* and *The Summer of 46*. The Rains returned to Holland in 1992 to continue their work with the Canadian war children of World War II. In 1997, Olga was awarded the Knights Cross by the Queen of the Netherlands for her volunteer work with Project Roots. Today, the Rains live in Haarlem, not far from where Olga grew up. They have three sons, ten grandchildren and six great-grandchildren of whom they are very proud.

Melynda Jarratt

Melynda Jarratt has her roots in New Brunswick, Canada, where she lives and runs her own information technology company. Melynda has a Bachelor of Arts (Honours History) and a Master of Arts in History from the University of New Brunswick in Fredericton. She also has a Diploma in Digital Media, which comes in handy as the webmaster of the Project Roots website (http://www.project-roots.com). Melynda has been involved with Project Roots since 1995, when she met Lloyd and Olga Rains through research she was conducting for her Master's thesis on the Canadian War Brides. Since then, Melynda has been involved in numerous history-related projects as a writer, researcher, filmmaker and web developer on projects ranging from Canada's History Television to the *Queen Mary II*. This book marks Melynda's entry into the world of publishing.